LOST

COLUMBIA COUNTY
NEW YORK

LOST
COLUMBIA COUNTY
NEW YORK

ALLISON GUERTIN MARCHESE

THE
History
PRESS

Published by The History Press
Charleston, SC
www.historypress.com

Copyright © 2025 by Allison Guertin Marchese

First published 2025

Manufactured in the United States

ISBN 9781467158008

Library of Congress Control Number: 2024947397

Notice: The information in this book is true and complete to the best of our knowledge. It is offered without guarantee on the part of the author or The History Press. The author and The History Press disclaim all liability in connection with the use of this book.

This book is dedicated to my parents, Lorraine Velardi Guertin and Alphé Albert John Guertin. We did not have much time together. You did not get to know me as a writer, a wife and a lover of horses and history, but you left me with an appreciation for the past. Thank you.

CONTENTS

ACKNOWLEDGEMENTS

I would like to acknowledge all of the people who understand the value of the beautiful place we call home, Columbia County, and work to preserve it. Mostly, I want to acknowledge those of us who believe in saving what is unique and irreplaceable. I want to thank you for not removing the unique bits of history that make our county so wonderful—the old wrought-iron fencing guarding the graves in the cemetery, the irreplaceable old church cornices, the fantastic historic moss-covered stone walls, the ancient shady maple trees, the rolling pastures and the dirt roads. If you love Columbia County's rural texture, history and beauty, then these are the remarkable pieces of our home that simply must survive. If we love our historic county, and want keep it that way, all of us must remain diligent and committed to preserving these special features. Don't lose sight of the reasons why we all moved here, why we stay here and why we live here. It's time to consider what each of us can do to keep Columbia County one of the most beautiful places in the world.

A special thanks goes out to Bruce Bohnsack for sharing his photos. Thanks to the Ghent Historical Society and to Albert Callan for his many years of writing amazing "Black Hat" stories in the *Chatham Courier*.

INTRODUCTION

Columbia County stretches from the Massachusetts border to the Hudson River. The county sits about a three-hour drive from New York City and two hours from Boston. Columbia County has a full-time population of 63,200 people. We share our county with plenty of cows, horses and sheep. Our major industry is still farming, with a few large dairy farms, apple orchards and large corn and hay fields.

Columbia County was officially formed in 1786 after the American Revolution. In total, Columbia County spreads across an area of 648 square miles, of which 635 square miles is land and 14 square miles is water.

The original inhabitants were Mohicans, an Algonquin people. Since 1609, the year Henry Hudson landed on our shores of the river that now bears his name, many souls have passed through Columbia County. Some of them remain unknown, yet some of them have been celebrated, like Aaron Burr, the famous character Ichabod Crane and President Martin Van Buren. Columbia County is notable. It boasts one of the oldest continuing New York State Fairs, dating back to 1841. And if you go back farther in time, you'll find that Columbia County has had many strange beasts travel the land. The first remains of a prehistoric mammal ever found, a molar and a hip bone of a mastodon, were discovered in Claverack in 1725.

In my first book, *Hidden History of Columbia County, New York* (The History Press, 2014), I included stories of these aforementioned pieces of history. Since publishing that book, I've been eager to write a "Part II" if you will. My second book, *Hudson Valley Curiosities* (The History Press, 2017), however, came next.

Since The History Press published *Curiosities*, several years have passed, COVID struck and my personal life took a few left turns with family members and illnesses, so writing a second installment of Columbia County history had to wait.

I've finally arrived at a place in time to write the book. *Lost Columbia County, New York* is here. In my research for this book, I stumbled on hundreds of amazing new history stories. Some of my favorites are collected in these pages. The chapters that follow vary from the unusual to the incredible, jaw-dropping history contained in the county's past. I do my best to recap the stories of several people, places and things have been lost to history. In addition, just for fun, I added a unique "Lost and Found" section in the book that reveals a variety of unusual history stories.

When I read about the county's history, I get totally absorbed, to the point that I sometimes feel like I'm time traveling. It's strange but true. I often feel like I'm right there, living and reliving the events of the past.

I've often struggled to find a single word that might convey the exact feeling I get when I delve into the past. Then one day I came across the Welsh word *hiraeth*. Eureka! There it was. Although the dictionary admittedly explains that there is no direct translation for *hiraeth*, the essence of the meaning of this beautiful and complex word is simply "homesickness." Yet there's more. The greater meaning of *hiraeth* tells us that it's used to capture deep internal longings and a desire to recapture something that has been lost. *Hiraeth* is meant to express a feeling of melancholy for a place or time that may never have existed or may have existed only in our minds. The word describes an intense longing to return to something—someone, somewhere or sometime. It's a tug on the heartstrings, I suppose. All the same, history, for me, is all about hiareth.

I guess questions arise then: Why should we care about the people, places and momentous events of earlier times? What does it matter that we live where once an Indian village was constructed or that some primeval forest once grew? Does a chronological sequence of what has occurred have any bearing on our world today? I say it does. Preserving the narrative, understanding the pioneers, clinging to the precious stories of the people in our past matters.

The story of Columbia County preserves our collective experience. There are lessons here involving fortitude, sacrifice, daring and greatness. If you travel around, look at the buildings, pick an apple off a tree or smell the cool air in late autumn, it's impossible to ignore the history. We have something to be grateful for—people, places and things that came before us. The next time you cross the Kinderhook Creek, gaze out at the Taghkanic mountain range, walk down Warren Street in the city of Hudson or discover a historic Dutch home, just take a moment to think about it. We are living in history and making our own history, placing our own unique signature on the place we call Columbia County.

Part I

LOST PEOPLE

THE SHAKERS' LOST EDEN: HEAVEN ON EARTH

What if Earth were truly the heaven we've all been waiting for? This was the thought of Ann Lee, the leader of the Shaker community, whose holy mountain is located in New Lebanon, New York.

Lee established a remarkable religious group with the belief that the kingdom of heaven was not some distant land beyond the stars in the cosmos, but rather right here on Earth. Ann was gifted in her ability to gather followers. She told her believers that she was, at last, the female reincarnation of Christ.

Ann, known as Mother Lee, taught the central idea that God is dual—both a male and a female, a father and a mother, and though she was never formally educated, Ann grasped this complex idea of the duality of God. Ann and her followers professed the astonishing belief that God manifested himself in the flesh, first in the male form as Christ and then in the female form in Ann. Ann wasn't the first to speak of this duality. Hindu theology, the oldest on earth, teaches that both male and female symbolize God.

What's odd is that Ann Lee was an unlikely person to lead a massive religious revival. She had a dreadful upbringing, an abusive marriage and a sordid past. Remarkably, it was only after Ann's death that the Shaker order she founded grew to tremendous numbers.

The Shaker movement began as a Protestant religious denomination officially called the United Society of Believers in Christ's Second Appearing, originating in Manchester, England, in 1747 in the home of Jane and James Wardley. The group was an offshoot of Quakerism. They were initially known as "Shaking Quakers" because of their ecstatic behavior during worship services.

In 1747, when Mother Ann Lee first met James Wardley, he was a preacher who maintained a small group of followers who had "possession by the spirit," much like many of the French prophets of the time.

It was August 6, 1774, when Ann Lee was driven out of England, persecuted for her religious beliefs. She and seven converts set out for New York to pursue their dreams of a utopian society. At that time, New York was simply a vast open wilderness of trees, streams and thick forests. It offered a fresh beginning and freedom to worship as they wished. The group first stayed in a town north of New York City (New Amsterdam) called Niskayuna, now known as Watervliet, near Albany.

Ann and her followers lived there, working and teaching until Ann died in 1784. Her gravestone still stands in the Shaker Cemetery in Colonie, New York. After their leader's death in Watervliet, the Shakers settled on Lebanon Mountain in New Lebanon, New York, in Columbia County, around the year 1789. The community took a large, beautiful tract of land on the mountain that cascades into the glorious New Lebanon valley below. They erected the "Society's" first church called the Mother Church and built their own homes, gardens and workshops.

The Shakers lived communally in the Mount Lebanon spiritual center, intentionally sequestering themselves away from society. They followed a spiritual path of purity and charity.

During her lifetime, Ann had many profound revelations. Among them was her belief that the root of human depravity was based in relations between men and women. Ann Lee also detested the notion of women in "servitude" under any circumstances, but especially in marriage. Therefore, the community of Shakers were celibate, with men and women living separately. The religious group was successful in attracting converts, however, and sometimes accepted married followers and their children to fortify their membership.

Ann believed that God saw men and women equally, therefore, leadership in the community was shared, although work was separate and men and women slept in different parts of the homes; they also worshiped in separate parts of the church, with separate entrances to buildings, separate seating at services and certainly no relationships allowed.

To the outside world, the Shakers were fascinating in many ways. They worked hard, and every aspect of their lives was a devotional act. What's even

Shakers members during worship. *New York Public Library Collections.*

more fascinating about the Shaker story is that the New Lebanon Shaker community still exists, and the Shaker influence on Columbia County is deep and lasting.

Charles Dickens was one of many influential people who visited the Shakers on the Mountain in New Lebanon. As was his way, he spoke his mind and had these harsh words: "They live in 'silent commonwealth' whose rigid rules 'strip life of its healthful graces, rob youth of innocent pleasures and make existence but a narrow path toward the grave.'"

The Shakers of New Lebanon focused on using spirit to drive their industries. They made all kinds of beautiful things, grew their own vegetables, made their own clothing, built farms and furniture and tools and even created one of the very first washing machines. Self-sufficiency was a daily practice.

Among the many things they invented was the idea of packaging garden seeds for sale. In fact, the first commercialized "seed packet" for home and farm use originated with the Shakers. Although the Shakers refused to participate in modern society and remained cloistered, they understood that to survive, they needed to make money.

One of their earliest businesses, starting in 1790, was packaging and selling seeds in bulk to local farmers. The New Lebanon Shakers actually did something that forever changed the way seeds were sold. The community of

Vintage Shakers seed box. *Library of Congress.*

Shakers at New Lebanon didn't just throw their precious seeds in a brown paper bag and send them off to customers; rather, they placed the purchased seeds in singular paper envelopes with colorful designs on the cover.

The Shakers set aside a portion of their land specifically to grow seeds for sale soon after settling in New Lebanon. While the Shakers felt that work and craftmanship was their way of worshiping God, the planting of seeds was a commercial endeavor and a way that they could meet the daily needs of the community. In fact, during the first part of the nineteenth century, the Shakers were one of a very few communities selling vegetable seeds to American home gardeners. The seed sales made up a major portion of the Shaker communities' income. The Shakers are thought to have developed the innovation of packaging seeds for sale in small paper packets. The first packets were cut and glued by hand in eight sizes. In New Lebanon, the packages included pound-bag size, bean size, beet size, onion size, cucumber size and so on.

By 1810, cutting and printing machines had been developed by the Shakers to speed up this process. The packets were boxed in decorative wooden display boxes. Some sales were made by mail-order catalogue, but most of the Shaker goods were sold by Shaker peddlers, who established routes throughout the northeastern United States. The group often used wagons packed with seed boxes, as well as herbs and herbal medicines, dried apples, brooms and other items they made themselves.

The group sold their goods, going from door to door, or provided the seeds to shops on consignment. They visited a number of surrounding rural communities, and that gave them an edge over other companies that had trouble reaching these families and farmers.

From this small cottage industry, the Shaker seed enterprise grew across the eastern part of the United States. Customers loved the quality of the seeds and reliability of the Shakers to deliver them. The New Lebanon community appears to have been one of the most successful overall—one of the longest-lived seed businesses and one of the most innovative. They came to refer to themselves in their advertisements as "The Shaker Seed Company." The overriding goal in all of the Shakers industries was "[t]he doctrine of perfectionism, the divinity of striving for excellence in every endeavor."

Shakers translated spiritual devotion into a strong work ethic. They were meticulous about every tiny detail in their daily activities. By striving for perfection, they believed that they were doing God's work. This ideal applied to everything from how they farmed, raising most of their own meat, vegetables and grain, to their beautifully built and well-crafted yet unadorned houses for themselves and their livestock. Although designs were considered "plain," the Shaker tools were as elegant as their furniture. The rule was to remain "simple."

This simple lifestyle applied to how they ate, their personal health, the clothes they wore and the things they made. Shakers of Columbia County made many items for sale. Despite their marketing advantages and efficiency of their seed business, the Shakers eventually were overwhelmed by larger seed production companies, which could manufacture bags and deploy an army of sales people. The Shakers also saw a steady decline in their membership.

At the communities' height in 1840, more than six thousand believers were still actively involved in nineteen Shaker villages spanning from New England to Ohio and south to Kentucky. At their peak, the Shakers were five thousand strong, with villages in Indiana all the way to Connecticut and from Maine to Florida. When the seven remaining Shakers left the North Family in 1947, Mount Lebanon was closed, and the last Shaker family in Columbia County, New York, ended.

The "Holy Mount" in New Lebanon, where the Shakers lived, is still open for tours by appointment.

"LOST" OF THE MOHICANS

Columbia County is rich with history, and with that history comes some sorrow and success. Columbia County was originally inhabited by the indigenous tribe known as the Mohican Indians. The Mohicans claimed (as also did other Indian tribes) that theirs was among the most ancient of all aboriginal nations.

As we know, Henry Hudson, an English explorer employed by the Dutch, sailed up the river that now bears his name. It was the year 1609. Columbia County was pure wilderness, and it was here that Henry Hudson stopped, anchored his vessel, the *Half-Moon*, and searched for food and supplies. He became the first white man to step foot on the land in our Columbia County.

While the ship was anchored, Mohican Indians boarded Hudson's ship and shared "fire-water." They "all drank until their tongues were loosened," said Captain Ellis, the author of *The History of Columbia County, 1857*. Captain Ellis described the scene: "It was not long before they again returned, and 'brought tobacco and beads,' which they presented to the captain [Hudson], and made an oration and showed him all the country round about." Soon after, the Mohicans brought back a platter of venison, which they ate together. Hudson was in awe at their Indian paradise.

After Hudson's historic stop, the Dutch were successful in creating a small settlement in Columbia County. They established a trading post, and eventually, New Amsterdam (New York City) took shape.

Later in the mid-1600s, Dutch colonists purchased land near Claverack, a word in Dutch that translates to "Clover Reach." By 1664, the English had taken over much of the Indian land. It was the last of these Woodland Period peoples, including the Algonquian-speaking Indians who resided in Columbia County. Sadly, by 1770, fewer than one hundred Mohicans remained in the county. However, from 1609, when Hudson landed in Columbia County, to about 1630, sometime before the Dutch settlement began, Mohican Indians lived on the land undisturbed.

In our county, scattered throughout miles of woodlands, there were many Mohican villages. The villages formed "sub-chieftaincies" under a variety of names. Their capitol was Es-ko-tak, near present-day Castleton. The name Es-ko-tak translates as "Place of the Ever Burning Fire." Other

Opposite: Mannessah historical marker. *Above*: Mohican tribe members. *Library of Congress.*

Mohican villages were located in Kinderhook, Stockport, Germantown and Claverack. One of the largest of all of the villages was called Potkoke and was situated on the Claverack Creek, known to the Indians as Twasta-wekak. The Mohican or Mohikan trail crossed Columbia County aligned with the present-day Route 23. This trail was known to the Indians as the Sunrise Path, as it followed east, just as the Sunset Path led west. Later, it was called the New England Path.

The Native Americans of Columbia County called themselves the Mhu-hik-kun-nuk, meaning "people of the continually flowing water." They used this word to describe the Hudson River because of its tidal action.

The Indian tribes of Columbia County lived under a democracy. They elected a chief, a sachem, at the "great meeting." They used "runners" to carry important messages from one village to another. These men were selected by the sachem. In the Mohican culture, women were given the right to vote along with men. This was true for all Eastern Indian tribes. In our own culture, it would take women until 1920 to gain the right to vote.

The Mohicans also had a custom of periodically abandoning their villages. This was done for a number of reasons, as when supplies like firewood and food ran low. When new villages were constructed, the Mohicans would pick a site that brought with it a fresh supply of dead trees for timber and saplings for building huts and sweat lodges. Indians did not need to build large elaborate homes. Most of their days were spent outdoors, so they chose simple furniture.

Most everything in the home was useful. After hunting elk, moose and deer, hides were used to make moccasins and clothing. Bear hides were cured to make fur bedding. Being a forest tribe, the Mohicans planted fields full of sweet corn. They also cultivated beans, squash, melon and pumpkins. As we know from stories, it was the Indians who first introduced these crops to the white settlers. Mohicans also gathered wild berries and nuts and tapped maple trees for sugar made from the rich sap that flowed through the trunks. To survive the long winters, Mohicans ate beaver meat in soup and used the beaver oils to make medicines. For a large part of the day, Mohicans would fish with nets or use a bone hook and a fiber line. Often the men would use harpoons to spear trout, salmon, pike and sturgeon.

In 1670, a council between New York governor Lovelace and Columbia County chiefs was assembled in Albany. The purpose of this remarkable meeting was to make peace between the English, who had taken over the governing of the area from the Dutch, and to settle differences between the rival Mohawk Indians and the Mohicans. With success in the air, all of the parties at the conference believed that the meeting marked the end of a long and brutal conflict between the two Indian tribes. It was also a great victory for the English, who would then employ them as allies and help them win several historic conflicts. While the Dutch relied on the Mohicans for fur trade, the English only had landownership on their mind, and the pressure on local Indians was relentless.

It's worth noting that it was the king of England who had previously given large tracts of land, or "manors," to his political friends like the Van Rensselaers and Livingstons in the New World. That meant the Livingston family were given generous amounts of land. Like the Dutch before them, the English gave only token items in trading for the massive area of property with the natives. In 1683 and again in 1685, Livingston purchased large areas from the Mohicans. The sale of the territory was known as Taghkanic and included Copake and Taghkanic Lakes. In return for giving up their homeland, the Indians received about $250 worth of wampum beads and about $250 in other goods. Wampum was a bead, fashioned out of the purple portions of a common clam shell or the spiral part of a snail's shell. At the time, when European currency was scarce, wampum was used as money.

The Indians resolved to move to a place that the whites had not yet discovered. They moved their council fire to Wa-nahk-ta-kock in the remote valley of the Housatonic.

After "selling their land" to Van Rensselaer and Robert Livingston, by natural migration, in 1770, there were fewer than one hundred Mohicans in Columbia County by the time of the American Revolution. It was then that the Mohicans helped the Americans, hoping that if a victory was secured, they could reclaim their lands and rights after being repeatedly denied by the British courts. Mohicans fought many times during the War of Independence and received a personal recommendation from General George Washington in a message to Congress. Daniel Nimham, their last chief, died as a hero in the Battle of White Plains in 1778. He along with many Mohicans gave their lives for the American cause and served Washington loyally as both scouts and messengers. The Mohicans were truly unselfish and a value to Washington.

There is a chapter in Columbia County's history of the Mohicans that may have been overlooked and almost lost. It involves a kind and lovely episode about a man on a mission.

Kaunameek, sometimes written as "Kannanmeek," was located at Brainard, New York, in the northeast corner of Columbia County near New Lebanon Valley. David Brainard was an Indian missionary in Columbia County. Where David Brainard settled, there was an Indian lodge on a high bluff on the edge of a beautiful valley spreading out over hundreds of acres with high mountains surging in the distance. Towering trees sheltered in native forests. These were the rich hunting grounds of the Indians that led to the lovely stream leading to Kaunameek, which might very well be the current-day Kinderhook Creek. The name means "sweet water," and the streams surrounding the area were rich with fish, a place where the native people felt safe and secure. Kaunameek was where David Brainard started his missionary work. In the present day, we can pinpoint this area near Route 66 north as it approaches Route 20 east.

Brainard arrived in April 1843 and spent about a year in this locale. He lived in a simple log hut that he built himself. It featured only a dirt floor and a bed made of straw and grass. For food, he ate boiled corn and "hasty pudding," which is a kind of mush containing cornmeal or wheat flour stirred into a thick batter in milk or water and was something like cream of wheat or oatmeal.

He spent a good amount of time in Stockbridge, where many Indians had migrated, and with Mrs. Sergeant, he studied the Mohican language. For this trip, he had to ride his horse back and forth many times over ten miles through wild country lacking in any roads, just crude paths in "primeval forests." These trips were hard and David endured the cold and stormy weather, but he did it with a cheerful heart, enduring the hardships knowing that he was doing what he loved.

In all, he spent a year at Kaunameek, learning the language of the Mohicans, studying their culture and ways and instructing them in religion. Later, many of the Mohicans moved to Stockbridge permanently and out of Columbia County.

The mission that David Brainard began would eventually dissolve, as the area grew with the influx of more white people and commerce. Remnants of David Brainard's time in the county remain.

Many years later, Brainard, New York, which straddles both Columbia and Rensselaer Counties, moved into a new era when busy stagecoaches stopped at well-established taverns and mills producing cotton and flannel made it an industrial center. In the early 1800s, Brainard became a bustling, energetic little village full of "enthusiasm for the future." Nearby, in the hamlet of Rayville, a religious sect, the Quakers, settled along the Kinderhook Creek. Within a few years, these industrious individuals had constructed a paper mill, a large woolen mill and a four-story cotton mill. The owner was named Gresham Turner. These mills created jobs for people who lived nearby and people who came from Lebanon Valley and East Nassau.

Stagecoaches traversed through Brainard daily throughout the nineteenth century, and a man named Major Benjamin Budd took advantage of the busy traffic and built a very large tavern on the west bank of the Kinderhook Creek. The tavern still stands today (though owned by a private family). In its original form, the Budd Tavern was a massive frame building constructed of local oak timber. On the second floor, there was a large ballroom where frequent dances were held for ladies and gentlemen of the countryside. In the main room of the tavern, a huge stone fireplace roared with a welcoming warmth, and mulled ale, roasted meat and fresh pies wafted from Dutch ovens in the expansive kitchen. Colonel Budd planted many large trees to shade the large barns built on the property to house the coach teams, which used the tavern as one of their regular stops. If you travel Route 20 from Nassau to New Lebanon, you'll still find the historical marker that pinpoints the tavern—the place where Budd Tavern still stands, away from the busy road, near the creek, beside the forest where the Mohican Indians camped, lived, listened to David Brainard's sermons and lived peacefully in our county, leaving their mark forever on our history.

ABE LINCOLN'S LOST BODY

One of the most tragic episodes in the course of the Civil War was the death of President Abraham Lincoln. He was assassinated on April 10, 1865, by John Wilkes Booth. One lesser-known fact is that Lincoln actually signed the bill creating what we know today as the Secret Service the exact same night he was shot at Ford's Theatre. The night of Lincoln's assassination, the president's bodyguard was curiously not at his post, but rather drinking at the saloon next door during intermission. The bodyguard was reportedly in the same saloon where John Wilkes Booth was also enjoying cocktails. One thing we know for sure is that the circumstances surrounding Lincoln's death and his body are strange—very strange.

In his life, Lincoln's physical body was described as being about six feet, four inches tall. His legs apparently seemed out of proportion with the rest of him, and when he sat in a chair, his knees rose up higher than his hips. When sitting in a chair, he often crossed his long legs or oddly threw them over the arms of the chair. Lincoln also had a habit of stooping forward when he stood, rounding his narrow shoulders, accentuating his painfully lean body.

Abraham Lincoln's hearse at Springfield, Illinois. *Library of Congress.*

His head was long, his forehead high and his ears stuck out at right angles from his head. Lincoln was often noted for his high cheekbones, his prominent brow and his sunken, staring, crisp blue eyes. And who can forget his rather long nose and protruding chin? He had an uncommonly big Adam's apple on his neck, and his hair was stiff and strange. People remarked that Lincoln's skin always looked a bit "leathery," which made it difficult to determine his age. The whole of Lincoln looked as if he was suffering.

After Lincoln's death, his body traveled in a special funeral train. Oddly, the *Lincoln Special* train car was built at Lincoln's request and delivered to the president in early 1865. Tragically, Lincoln never rode in it until his death.

During the aftermath of his assassination, Lincoln's body lay in state at the White House and the rotunda of the Capitol before being loaded into the railroad car. In another strange twist, the specially built train car had to be modified to transport Lincoln's coffin and the coffin of his beloved, eleven-year-old son, Willie, who had died of typhoid fever in 1862 during the Civil War. Willie had previously been buried at Georgetown's Oak Hill Cemetery, but after his father's assassination, his coffin was removed and placed aboard the funeral train.

The funeral train carrying Abe and his son traveled from Washington, D.C., to New York, through Columbia County, stopped briefly in Hudson and Stuyvesant and then moved on to Albany on its way west to its final destination in Springfield, Illinois.

The infamous train carrying the remains of President Abraham Lincoln left Washington, D.C., on April 20, 1865, a week after the assassination. Oddly, and with much criticism, Lincoln's wife, Mary Todd Lincoln, did not ride in the train with her dead husband and deceased son. Having witnessed the assassination, her dress splattered with blood, Mary was too distraught to leave her room and missed the funeral altogether.

On a twelve-day journey to Springfield, Illinois, Lincoln's train stopped in Hudson, New York, on April 25, 1865. The journey toward Hudson began when the train left New York City at 4:15 p.m. on April 25. The train chugged along the edge of the Hudson River and made its slow procession into Columbia County:

> *Along the sides of the rural route were throngs of mourners gathered like lost flocks of birds along the river's edges. They came from miles away just to stand along silent dirt roads. They waited patiently, just to catch a glimpse of the passing train and to say their final farewell to the man who has preserved democracy and ended slavery.*

The Lincoln
hearse arch
at 12th Street,
Chicago.
*Library of
Congress.*

When the locomotive finally arrived in Hudson, thousands of local citizens came out to meet it. It was the practice of the officials who accompanied the president's body to remove Lincoln's coffin when it arrived in a city and carry it in a grand procession to a place where it would lie in state, to be viewed by masses of faithful mourners. In New York City, the casket traveled by hearse to the rotunda at city hall. A reporter noted, "The catafalque graced the principal entrance to the Governor's Room. Its form was square, but it was surmounted by a towering gothic arch, from which folds of crape, ornamented by festoons of silver lace and cords and tassels, fell artistically over the curtained pillars which gave form and beauty to the structure."

On the day Lincoln's dead body arrived in Hudson, people waited along the streets until 9:45 p.m. By this late hour, more than two thousand people had gathered near the waterfront station to see the train pull in. Assistant Adjutant General Edward D. Townsend, commander of the funeral train, recorded what transpired:

> *At Hudson…elaborate preparations had been made. Beneath an arch hung with black and white drapery and evergreen wreaths, was a tableau representing a coffin resting upon a dais; a female figure in white mourning over the coffin; a soldier standing at one end and a sailor at the other. While*

a band of young women dressed in white sang a dirge, two others in black entered the funeral-car, placed a floral device on the President's coffin, then knelt for a moment of silence, and quietly withdrew. This whole scene was one of the most weird ever witnessed, its solemnity being intensified by the somber light of the torches at that dead hour of night.

Although Lincoln passed briefly through Columbia County on the way back to his final resting place, this was by no means the famous emancipator's only touch with our region. A strange set of coincidences, a brush with fate and a ghostly tale all surround the story of Lincoln and Columbia County.

Before Lincoln was the "great emancipator," the president-elect visited the region. He made a stop in Albany to address the State Assembly. Lincoln also made contact with our region when he donated an original handwritten draft of the Emancipation Proclamation to the Albany Army Relief Bazaar in 1865. The original full draft was lost in the great Chicago Fire; however, a few women of Albany were planning an Army Relief Bazaar in Academy Park to raise funds for the C.S. Sanitary Commission, a forerunner of the Red Cross. They wrote to the president asking him for some articles that could be auctioned off, and he sent them the Proclamation draft. Tickets were sold on it and brought $1,100. The winner, however, returned it to the ladies of the bazaar, and one year later, it was purchased for the State of New York by the legislature for $1,000.

Lincoln had another interesting encounter in the region when he happened to meet his assassin purely by coincidence. In yet another bizarre encounter, a correspondent in the Albany, New York *Evening Times* related a conversation with a superstitious night watchman on the New York Central Railroad. Said the watchman:

"I believe in spirits and ghosts. I know such things exist. If you will come up in April I will convince you." He then told of the phantom train that every year comes up the road with the body of Abraham Lincoln. Regularly in the month of April, about midnight, the air on the track becomes very keen and cutting. On either side it is warm and still. Every watchman when he feels this air steps off the track and sits down to watch. Soon after the pilot engine, with long black streamers, and a band of black instruments, playing dirges, grinning skeletons sitting all about, will pass up noiselessly, and the very air grows black. If it is moonlight clouds always come over the moon, and the music seems to linger, as if frozen with horror. A few moments after and the

phantom train glides by. Flags and streamers hang about. The track ahead seems covered with black carpet, and the wheels are draped with the same. The coffin of the murdered Lincoln is seen lying on the centre of the car, and all about it in the air and the train behind are vast numbers of blue-coated men, some with coffins on their backs, others leaning on them.

What's even most curious about Abraham Lincoln is his visit through Chatham. After delivering a speech in Boston in September 1848, Lincoln passed through Chatham on his way to Albany basically unnoticed. In that year, Lincoln was not considered an expert orator. In fact, the official newspaper reported that the *Whig* did not reprint a line from any of his speeches made that fall, and few knew the name Abraham Lincoln. Lincoln did, however, severely criticize Martin Van Buren in that Boston speech. Lincoln would detrain at Rensselaer and take a ferry across to Albany, where he was scheduled to see Thurlow Weed. Later, the two were planning a visit to Millard Filmore.

But what's most haunting about Lincoln's connection to Columbia County concerns the night after the taking of Richmond, at the close of the Civil War. Sister Celia De Vere, of the Mount Lebanon Shakers, in a dream, witnessed the assassination of President Lincoln. She related it to the other Shakers, and eleven days later, the prophesied message of the murder reached Mount Lebanon, according to Lester Gifford's historical sketches. In February 1862, one year into the Civil War, a twenty-five-year-old Shaker woman named Sister Cecilia De Vere lay asleep in her bed. The prosperous village of Mount Lebanon, New York, was far away from the carnage taking place farther south, yet Sister Cecilia's dreams were troubled. Suddenly, she began to sing a song no one had ever heard before. We now know the song as "Supplication in a Nation's Calamity," or "Prayer for the Captive." Three years after Cecilia first sang "Supplication," Shaker villages across the country would sing it to honor Lincoln after he was assassinated.

HENRY HUDSON: LOST AT SEA

Little is known about Henry Hudson's early life, and as this story will reveal, little is known about the end of his life. We know for certain that Henry Hudson was English, and according to a few sources, the name Hudson was associated with voyages to the Arctic around 1585 in search of a Northwest Passage from Europe to Asia. It is thought that Thomas Hudson, perhaps a relative, contributed to the planning of an early voyage and that Henry Hudson might have been present during that planning, hence his interest in exploration of the Arctic.

One thing is for certain: Henry Hudson had a thorough knowledge of Arctic geography. Two wealthy companies thought enough of him to invest in him to navigate their ships.

The voyage that Henry Hudson took in the spring of 1609 is the one that has impacted our region of Columbia County the most. After two previous voyages in search of passage to Japan and China by way of the Arctic, Hudson was hired by the Dutch East India Company. He began in Holland, boarding his ship, the *Half-Moon*, on April 6, 1609. While in Amsterdam preparing for the trip, Hudson had heard reports of two possible channels to the Pacific across North American. One such passage was recorded by the English explorer and colonist Captain John Smith, who was well known as the leader of the Jamestown Colony, the first permanent English settlement in the New World.

Once the voyage was underway, Hudson and his crew experienced terrible storms and impossible headwinds. Instead of returning, he and his men decided to carry on, seeking the Northwest Passage previously sought by Smith.

Cruising along the Atlantic coast, Hudson encountered the river we now know by his name. He traveled the river for about 150 miles until he reached Albany, New York. Once there, he was resigned to the fact that the river would never lead to the Pacific Ocean. He returned to Holland with his report, yet Hudson was not satisfied. He set out on another voyage, determined to find a way to the Pacific.

Hudson left London in April 1610 on the ship *Discovery* with a brief stop in Iceland. He then proceeded to the Baffin Island's north shore into a place where he was to find "Furious Overfall," which he renamed Hudson Bay. He passed through Hudson Bay in early August and then traveled south, finding himself in James Bay with no outlet at all. It was

Henry Hudson set adrift. *Library of Congress.*

Henry Hudson stone, with the initials found in the stone. *Library of Congress.*

then that Hudson refused to give up and simply rode around without any sense of a plan until, finally, winter weather caught up with him and the crew. Early in 1611, experiencing an Arctic winter, his men became restless and anxious. There were rumors that Hudson was hoarding food and that, combined with frigid temperatures, the men on the ship became enraged. As floes surrounded the ship, Robert Juet, the mate, was demoted. At that moment, mutiny rose in the ranks.

Abacuk Prickett, one of the only literate members of the crew, kept a diary and described the situation: "It was a labyrinth without end...We had a storm and the wind brought the ice so fast upon us, that it in the end we were driven to put her inot the chiefest of the ice, and there to let her lie. Some of our men this day fell sicke, I will not say it was for feare, although I saw small signs of other griefe."

Hudson was desperate to find a southern outlet back to the Atlantic Ocean, but his men wanted to try a northern route seeking open water. More ice circled the boat until the *Discovery* became trapped. The men were forced to haul the ship ashore and experienced a punishing winter in that place, stuck in the ice with no contact from the outside world. On June 22, 1611, Juet conspired with others, and on the voyage home, mutineers seized Henry Hudson and his son and, with seven others, sent them adrift in a small open boat.

The *Discovery* successfully sailed home to England, and the crew was tried for mutiny. Four men were tried for the murder of their captain, but they were acquitted. They blamed the mutiny on the crew who had died on the passage home. As for Henry Hudson, his son, John, and the others cast adrift, they were never heard from again.

In all, Henry Hudson took on four very dangerous voyages, brought his ships and crew through Arctic winters and somehow saved all of his vessels from harm.

The same, however, does not hold true for poor Henry Hudson. It's now been more than four hundred years since Henry Hudson went missing. Many theories about his fate have bubbled up over the years. One such theory is centered on the town of Chalk River, Ontario, Canada, where an unusual stone was uncovered by a road worker paving crew in 1959. On the stone is carved the initials "HH" with the date 1612 and a few words: "held captive." We may never know what truly happened to old HH, but we here in Columbia County will remember him well.

LOST PIRATE HERO: WILLIAM HENRY ALLEN

If you want to understand the history of lost souls from the ground up, so to speak, look no further than the history of cemeteries in Columbia County—and the mysteries of the people who are buried there. Cemeteries have a unique way of tugging on our curiosities. They pull us in with invisible silver strings and beg us to walk among the almost parklike settings. It's not often that we jog or drive past a cemetery and fail to stare and wonder. What lurks in there? Better yet, who?

According to *The History of Columbia County, New York* by Captain Franklin Ellis, "Along the northeaster declivity of Prospect hill, and extending down to the Old Columbia Turnpike, lies the ground of the Hudson cemetery; a spot combining all the requisites that enlighten modern taste demands in a place of graves,—rural quiet, great natural beauty and a conformation of surface peculiarly adapted to receive those artificial embellishments which sore-hearted mourners love to lavish around the resting-places of their dead."

The Cedar Park Cemetery is located on the outskirts of the city of Hudson in Columbia County. One of its inhabitants is none other than William Henry Allen, the man for whom Allen Street in Hudson is named. William Henry Allen's gravestone reads as follows:

> Pride of his country's banded chivalry,
> His fame their hope, his name their battle cry;
> He lived as mothers wish their sons to live,
> He died as fathers wish their sons to die.
> Fitz Greene Halleck

To most, William Henry Allen was a local hero, a lieutenant in the U.S. Navy. In short, Allen fell a martyr in service of his country. He was born in the city of Hudson on July 8, 1790, and he was killed while in command of the U.S. schooner *Alligator*.

W<u>m</u>. Henry. Allen Esq.

late of the United States Navy.

William Henry Allen portrait. *Library of Congress.*

If you've walked through the city of Hudson, you know that Allen Street is a place of elaborate homes with stunning architecture; they carry history in their walls. William Henry Allen was a true native son, born to a fine family. History tells us that his family was of means. As a small child, he spent part of 1798 at boarding school in London, England. He then returned home, studied in the city of Hudson at the local Academy for Boys in the early 1800s and then his education was completed at the seminary in Doylestown, Pennsylvania.

Allen put his extensive skills to work in the navy, leading his men with intelligence, patience and expert precision. His career was impressive by anyone's standards. And in Allen's case, he was far braver than most men in uniform. After being appointed midshipman in the U.S. Navy in 1808, he became a second lieutenant in 1811. While fighting in the War of 1812, he served aboard the USS *Argus* and was wounded, losing a leg. It was the first time Allen became a hero.

On August 14, 1813, in a battle with the British sloop of war *Pelican*, he was taken prisoner and served eighteen months as a prisoner of war in Ashburton, England. On August 3, 1822, as commander of the schooner *Alligator*, while cruising the Caribbean near Cuba, Allen set out in search of pirates. His mission was to eradicate the ongoing marauding of U.S. fleets. Soon after arriving in Havana, he learned that a gang of pirates in possession of some merchant vessels were stationed in the bay of Le Juapo near Matanzas. The pirates were holding five merchant men and several American citizens hostage.

Approaching, Allen observed three pirate ships, well armed and manned by more than one hundred murderous thieves. Although it was dangerous for the *Alligator* to get close enough due to the shallow waters, Allen ordered his long boats to be lowered and with the help of thirty crew boarded the pirate ship, determined to rescue the hostages. The fight was ferocious, and the Americans fought desperately for their lives. Allen was successful in taking control of the vessel, causing the outlaws to flee, but during the course of the musket fire, he was wounded. Miraculously, although Allen took a shot to the head, he continued to move forward, fighting for his crew. Just when he was about to board the very last enemy ship, Allen was hit a second time. This time the shot penetrated his torso. A musket ball pierced his heart directly.

Allen's men carried him away from the ship and to safety. Despite every effort to stave off the bleeding, Lieutenant William Henry Allen died later that day. Those around him said that minutes before his death, although his pain must have been overwhelming, he was talking jovially with his crew and seemed at peace with his decisions. Although his remains were first buried at Matanzas on November 11, 1822, they were later exhumed and buried in Hudson.

On December 15, 1827, the schooner *Grampus* arrived in New York City with the body of the hero William Henry Allen. John Edmonds, a Hudson attorney and judge, along with Rufus Reed of the Hudson Common Council, headed a special committee and met the ship as it glided into the wharf.

Escorted by the Marine Corps in New York City, the body left the Brooklyn Navy Yard and was taken by steamboat to its final resting spot in Hudson. Cannons fired and bells tolled in Hudson in honor of the return of the city's native son. The ashes of Allen are at rest at the Hudson cemetery beneath a marble monument with this inscription: "To the memory of William Henry Allen, Lieutenant in the United States navy who was killed when in the act of boarding a piratical vessel on the coast of Cuba, near Matanzas at the age of thirty-two."

LOST ACTORS OF MALDEN BRIDGE

If you've never heard of Malden Bridge, a hamlet of Chatham, New York, you're not alone. It would also stand to reason that an even smaller percentage of people have heard of the Malden Bridge Playhouse. Here is some history.

In 1931, a vibrant new establishment was added to the canvas of Columbia County. A school for teaching theater techniques came to life in Malden Bridge. It was originally called the Berkshire Theater Workshop but soon became known as the Bishop Lee School of the Theatre in Boston.

The managers were Ms. Adele Hoes Lee and Emily Paree Nietche. Mrs. Hoes Lee's grandfather Robert Hoes was inventor of the Columbian pump. She became the wife of Charles Lee, who formerly owned a pump company on the site of the new playhouse. Established in 1824, Robert Hoes Company Inc. manufactured the Thayer's Columbia pump, recognized as a pump that "stood the test of time" for eighty years. In 1923, the owners—Robert Hoes, his son, Guy M. Hoes and Charles Lee—moved the pump company to Church Street in Chatham. As an interesting aside, Robert Hoes was also one of the grand jurors who indicted Oscar Beckwith at his murder trial.

Ms. Hoes Lee, who was married to Charles Lee, apparently had a vision for the old factory and the barns in Malden Bridge and created the drama school. Mrs. Lee was a Columbia County native. She and her husband moved to the area from Detroit, Michigan. Adele had grown up in Chatham. All through her life, Adele Lee had a passion for singing and acting and would frequently give performances and recitals in the local churches and halls. In 1931, Mrs. Lee's dream of opening a drama school was realized, and the very first "workshop" included twenty-two young women who brought with them some stage experience. The school stated its mission publicly in the local newspaper. The group intended to "render several dramatic productions during the summer, these to be staged as soon as the course of training has progressed to a point satisfactory to the heads of the school."

A few months later that year, the group debuted at a performance. Quite by coincidence, the play happened to be one of Edna St. Vincent Millay's called *The King's Henchman*. The performers would later offer a second drama called *Gypsy Fires*, which was staged at the auditorium of the Chatham High School. All subsequent performances were held at the playhouse barns.

When it first opened, the drama school was known by yet another name: the Nell Gwyn Theater. But into the 1940s, the theater closed for the duration of World War II. In 1941, Mrs. Lee became involved in the war effort. The theater changed hands and was reopened under new management in 1946, called the Malden Bridge Playhouse. Although not shining stars, the actors and actresses appearing at the Malden Bridge Playhouse were somewhat celebrated and came from around the country. A core group seemed to come back in the summers year after year, among whom were Paul Broussard, Arthur Gorton, Betty Parker, Robert Hartman and John Hale.

By 1957, the Malden Bridge Playhouse had undergone some extensive renovations and was a sturdy, 250-seat professional summer stock theater sitting on a dirt road along a simple stream in an out-of-the-way hamlet three hours from New York City.

Despite its remote location, the theater became a place where celebrities of our time paid their play-acting dues in summer stock performances. One such actor was Barbra Streisand.

Barbra Streisand at the Malden Bridge Playhouse. *Matte Howe.*

During the summer of 1957, Barbra slyly lied to her mother so that she could get enough money to run away from home to join a group of apprentices at the Malden Bridge Playhouse in Columbia County, New York. Her first experience on the stage, however, turned out to be scrubbing floors, painting sets and doing other chores at the little rural theater. In her biography, she said, "By the time I was fourteen, I wanted to get into summer stock. During my school vacation the next year, I went to a playhouse upstate with one hundred and fifty dollars my mother gave me. Later I found it was really money that my grandfather had left me," Streisand recalled. "I had a wonderful time at the playhouse," she said. "I played in *Picnic*, and was one of the sexy girls in *The Desk Set*."

In an old twelfth season program from the play *Death of a Salesman*, there in the list of staff you can see Barbra Streisand's name listed under "properties," along with stagehands and among advertisements for the Bonfire and the Cabin Restaurants on Route 66.

For convenience, the actors of the Malden Bridge Playhouse stayed directly across the street from the theater in a rustic-style lodge. Barbra said that the summer she acted at the theater, she roomed with Ingrid Meighan, who remembered Streisand as having "a wonderful sense of humor and was more of a comic than a serious actor."

The lodge was converted from the old pump factory. It also served as the rehearsal hall, a work space for scenery construction and wardrobe fittings. At the time, the lodge was considered as upscale accommodations compared to the pre-fab chicken coops (like Sears and Roebuck houses arriving in the mail) that often housed some of the actors.

The *Chatham Courier*'s review of Ms. Streisand's first speaking role in *The Desk Set* noted that she "turns in a fine performance as the office vamp—Down Boys!" Although Barbra played in a few additional minor roles that year, she never returned to the Malden Bridge Playhouse. After three decades of summer stock, the theater closed around 1961.

Circling back in the 1960s, Mrs. Hoes Lee had what you could call a second act in Malden Bridge. Joining forces with another Malden Bridge resident, Mrs. Aimes, the two women founded the Malden Bridge Arts and Crafts Center in what is now a home and a space that houses the post office.

Previously, the building represented Malden Bridge's "town center." In the mid-1800s, the central part of the building held a general store. Before that, it was a Baptist church with one wing serving as a parsonage. The second floor was once a private Episcopal chapel for the prominent Peaseley family, whose straw paper mill dominated the hamlet. The area once used as a residence is where Lee and Aimes created the arts and crafts center. They outfitted the rooms with large antique white oak tables where they displayed everything from hand-knitted sweaters to local ceramics, paintings, woven towels and hand-loomed fabrics. Mrs. Lee even installed her own loom, on which she demonstrated weaving to customers. She was especially known for her special "tote bags" and her braided rugs on the floor. She hooked a rug depicting the hamlet of Malden Bridge, her family home. The women came up with the idea for the arts and crafts store on their own and did all the work themselves.

As long as we're going down the road of arts and theater in Malden Bridge, it's worth noting that in 1960, Louis Bouche, an Old Chatham summer resident, a member of the national academy and a world-renowned artist, donated a painting to a charity festival at St. Joseph's church (now the Malden Bridge Community Center). At the time, the painting was appraised at $1,200.

The annual festival, though in a tiny little church, attracted a lot of people of all faiths. The interfaith relationships among people from Malden Bridge, Rider's Mills and Old Chatham area were carrying on a long tradition. In fact, it was the Protestants who gave to the founders of St. Joseph's Roman Catholic Church their site in Malden Bridge. Horace W. Peaslee, one of the owners of the paper mill in Malden Bridge, conveyed the parcel of land to St. Joseph's on November 28, 1871. According to the deed, the conveyance was a gift to be used for a church and nothing else. The small plot of land was part of the farmlands situated across the Kinderhook Creek from the Peaslee residence, which was later occupied by Mr. and Mrs. Francis Aimes. In the years after the Civil War, Catholic families moved into the area, followed by a group of Quakers. In those days, Catholic families had to travel on foot or by horse or carriage to Valatie to attend Mass. That all changed in 1871. Louis Bouche's painting memorialized this church. The original painting is still owned by a resident of Malden Bridge.

Part II

LOST PLACES

LOST LAKES AND FDR'S SCENIC PARKWAY

Anyone who travels through Columbia County naturally slows down a bit when they see the beauty of the expansive waterways that dot the landscape. Who wouldn't want to gaze at the soft, rippling water hidden behind sweeping pines and laid against yellow meadow grass. No one could imagine the countryside without the beauty of the willows brushing the small streams and ponds.

In the history of the county, many things have survived the test of time, including our lakes. In Columbia County, there are four special lakes: Queechy Lake in Canaan, Kinderhook Lake in Niverville, Copake Lake in Copake and Lake Taghkanic. The area is one of the original Livingston family grants and was formerly a part of the Livingston manor. The family name dates back hundreds of years in Columbia County.

Lake Taghkanic sits in a state park and is probably the last of the publicly accessible places where anyone can partake in the outdoor beauty and touch a toe down in the brisk, cool waters. Taghkanic State Park is the work of a man very dear to our county: Franklin D. Roosevelt.

As most know, Franklin Roosevelt was a native of Hyde Park, New York, which is located about thirty miles from Lake Taghkanic. In 1910, Roosevelt was running for the New York State Senate, and he spent much of his time traversing by car, visiting area landmarks and making speeches in Dutchess County and Columbia County while he was securing his seat. In this era, cars were not very reliable and roads were less than smooth, so traveling through the county took quite a bit of time and effort. Roosevelt was known for stopping at Taghkanic Lake both while growing up in the area and while running for office, and in 1925, he was appointed the very first chairman of the Taconic State Park Commission by the governor.

It was Roosevelt's job to assess if the lake region could become a New York state park. To our good luck, Roosevelt indeed decided that the lake would make a superb park, and he added that he could create a scenic parkway for travelers to get there (now known as the Taconic Parkway). Roosevelt's plan was no less than brilliant. The parkway was planned to be a beautiful way to travel through the eastern portion of the Hudson Valley. He wanted everyone to experience the stunning overlooks, the views of the Catskill Mountains and the amazing trees and forests that line the path. Roosevelt designed the parkway to pass near to the lovely Lake Taghkanic.

Before adopting its new name, Lake Taghkanic was called Lake Charlotte after an enslaved person who served the famous Livingston family. In the early days, locals knew the name not as "char-lott" but rather pronounced it "sha-lott." At some point, the local residents called the waterway "Cobi's Pond."

In its heyday in the 1900s, Lake Charlotte was a huge gathering place. Buses would leave Warren Street on Sunday morning to transport picnickers and swimmers at a cost of one dollar per trip. The Rockefeller family held meetings at Lake Charlotte. A newspaper notice read, "The Rockefeller Family Association, which was organized in Germantown, N. Y., in 1905 and has since then steadily increased its membership until now it is nearly four hundred, will hold a meeting at Lake Charlotte—in, Columbia county on Tuesday, August 28th, 1923. All Rockefellers and descendants of Rockefellers are invited to attend the box or basket picnic and are urged to participate in the entertainment that will be provided."

The trout fishing was quite amazing, and swimming at the lake was one of the most popular activities. In the early 1900s, people rode their horses to the waterfront to take a dip. Dances took place at Wentzel's pavilion on Saturday evenings at Lake Charlotte with Professor Bud Long leading the orchestra.

Small, simple summer cottages lined the shores. Some were nothing more than shacks, with teetering porches and screen windows. At one point, there were two taverns on the lake, one of which was known as "Seven Sisters." Locals say that it survived until the 1950s and that its bar and dance floor were still quite lively. The dance area had a second function. On Sundays, the Catholic church would hold service there, provided by a priest from Germantown. In the summer, the local farmers would ride to

Taghkanic State Park, 1956.
Library of Congress.

Lake Charlotte in horse-drawn carriages to sell fruits and vegetables. This went on late into the 1940s.

In 1929, Lake Charlotte was then a privately owned lake, and the owner, Dr. McRae Livingston, was ready to sell. His first stop on his mission to find a buyer was a visit to a member of the Taconic State Park Commission to ask if it would be interested in buying the lake and the surrounding property. By then, FDR had been replaced. Livingston was willing to offer the entire 255-acre lake and all six miles of the shoreline and an additional 172 acres of land for little or no money. The asking price was a mere $25,000. In 1930, they sealed the deal, and the property was officially transferred to the commission. Livingston's only condition was that the lake be changed from Charlotte to Lake Taghkanic, a Algonquian word meaning either "enough water" or "lots of wood" (depending on which translation you prefer). The sale of the land was the end of lakeside simple cottages, as the Civilian Conservation Corps arrived to start turning the property into a state park.

As part of FDR's New Deal to put people back to work after the Great Depression, he again took an interest in how the new Taghkanic Park would look. Part of the plan was to have the CCC build a new beach, bathhouse and freshwater system, including a fifty-foot-high stone storage tower. The organization also wove hiking trails into the heavily wooded areas surrounding three quarters of the lake and added a number of camping sites; it also converted some of the old cottages left standing into summer rentals.

The new park made its debut in 1934. The main entrance faces Route 82, and although money was scarce in 1934, locals were required to pay a fee to get in. For almost ten years, throughout World War II and the Depression that followed, the park had few improvements. In 1945, at the end of the war, the plan that FDR had started in 1925 to see a scenic parkway built was finally revived.

In 1954, the Taconic State Parkway opened between Route 199 in Dutchess County and Route 82 in Columbia County. One of the most exciting features of the new roadway was an exit into Lake Taghkanic State Park. The park was therefore an easy day trip from any point south, which meant weekenders and vacationers coming from New York City grew by the hundreds, just like FDR had hoped.

The good news was that FDR's dreams were realized. The bad news was that the park soon became overcrowded. The answer to the overcrowding was to start constructing a second beach on the west end of the lake, along with a large bathhouse complete with a locker room. Also added was a concession stand with outdoor patio seating and a new parking lot with the capacity for thousands of cars. The boathouse offered rentals for the day, and a large green grassy area was installed for picnics, softball games and other activities. To accommodate the crowds, more hiking trails were designed, along with additional roads.

Today, the park still reflects the atmosphere of a 1950s camp. Plans in the 1960s for a skating rink, ski slopes, a lodge and a world-class golf course never got off the ground. Today, Lake Taghkanic is open year-round for day use activities. Overnight camping is available May through October. A daily vehicle use fee is charged seasonally. Winter activities include ice fishing, cross-country skiing, snowshoeing, snowmobiling and ice skating.

As so many people enjoy the excitement of the Taghkanic Lake and the public park, in years past, Taghkanic had a romantic appeal. As it was once written:

> *Paramount beauty prevails at Lake Charlotte. In fact, this is the time of the season when the splendors of the neighborhood are seen to greatest advantage; the time when nature's colors seem to harmonize better. Those who have never witnessed a sunset or the rising of a harvest moon at Lake Charlotte have missed a picture no artists could depict and no writer describe with the vivid style necessary to awaken with one's bosom that thrill that keen love for God's green earth, which seems to imbue one who becomes fascinated by nature's beauties. Quiet, serene and picturesque. In those few words you*

have the surroundings here in a nutshell, but there are numerous but there are numerous sidelights, so to speak, about which one could write for hours. The rich aroma of the new mown hay, the cool breeze that seems to exist all the time, the song of the tall pines at the east side, the healthful air and good water—all of which gives the lake an attractiveness that appeals to man, woman and child. It might truly be said that Gallatin has a paradise.

LOST SODA FOUNTAINS AND ICE CREAM PARLORS

Is the ice cream parlor a thing of the past—lost to time? Maybe not. Back in the 1950s, residents of Columbia County could buy a quart of ice cream for forty-five cents and free delivery service if you purchased in "gallon quantities, within a reasonable distance."

Due to the high dairy content, believe it or not, ice cream was promoted in the '50s as a healthy and wholesome product, along with being fun to eat. Brick Ice Cream shop, located in the neighboring Berkshires, was one of the leading manufacturers of high-grade ice cream. The company was a big hit locally and served ice cream at parties, banquets and weddings. In addition to making the ice cream on site, Brick boasted an ice cream parlor, which in essence was a modern little lunchroom with spit-shine-polished, stainless steel surfaces and bright, cheerful lights. The most notable feature of the ice cream parlor was the service. Mrs. Patton ran the ice cream parlor in Valatie and at Kinderhook Lake, one of the most noted ice cream parlors at the former Electric Park.

Old Boston candy shop, Chatham, New York. *New York Public Library Collection.*

In the 1930s, you could find an ice cream shop in every town and village in Columbia County. The milk for the ice cream was provided by local Columbia County dairy farmers, and some of the farms had their own ice cream or "dairy bars" right on the property so that you could pet the cows on your way in to buy a cone.

Foiadelli's on Main Street in Chatham was famous for its "triple decker cone," for just ten cents, with the cream made by Velvet the cow at the Normanskill farm dairy. Foiadelli's also offered Eskimo Pies, Eskimo Fugies and Creamsicles, a combination of orange and vanilla ice cream on a stick. The proprietors of Foiadelli's also encouraged buyers to "save the wrapper's" on their cones, where they would print special coupons and giveaways.

Baker Brothers on Austerlitz Street in Chatham advertised its own special recipe for homemade peach ice cream and offered special "Jumbo Peach sodas" for fifteen cents. Baker's also boasted the only ice cream delivery service in town.

Lant's Ice Cream Shop was on the family farm in East Chatham and gave customers the unique opportunity to "drive up," sit on the lawn or take a seat at a table right in its own kitchen!

Miller's in Ghent owned an ice cream stand. The little roadside stop was famous for its "candy tobacco" and banana splits. It's worth digressing a bit here to give a bit of background on the invention of the banana split. The original banana split was made with three scoops of ice cream, topped with fruit (like strawberries) and served over a banana that was cut vertically down the middle. Sometimes the dish was served with crushed pineapple and raspberries and even black cherries. The whole delicious concoction was sprinkled with chopped nuts and even some homemade marshmallow; chocolate syrup was slathered over the length of the dessert, which was finished off with whipped cream and a big red cherry. Most shops served the dessert in a long, boat-shaped glass bowl. Credit for the invention of the banana split is customarily given to a twenty-three-year old pharmacy clerk at Tassell's Pharmacy from Latrobe, Pennsylvania, named David Strickler. Strickler was challenged one day to make something different. Bananas were relatively new imports in the States at that time in 1904. Having already eaten plenty of ice cream sundaes in his time, he made this culinary creation. Just for the record, pouring syrups on ice cream wasn't entirely new—Thomas Jefferson was fond of pouring maple syrup over top of his favorite flavors.

History has it that people traveled from all Massachusetts and beyond to visit Barden's in Spencertown for ten-cent cones with two large scoops of its eight homemade flavors. A short drive outside of Chatham, you'd find Ostrander's ice cream stand in one direction and Strever's in another.

Probably the most notable of all of the ice cream "shoppes" was the Boston Candy Kitchen in the center of Chatham on Main Street. Each morning, Nick Demos, the owner and manager of the store, made the ice cream himself. Nick liked to invite people to come and watch the process.

Making ice cream at the turn of the century. *Library of Congress.*

Patrons could sit in the ice cream parlor and soda fountain and enjoy a cone or a sundae made with the freshly made ice cream.

For anyone who thinks that ice cream parlors and shops might be kind of ho-hum news, there's a bit of history you might want to know. In the 1800s, ice was considered a luxury. You heard that right. To keep your food cold in the hot weather, companies made an entire business out of harvested ice in the winter, cutting it from local lakes and ponds, storing it and then selling it to households and farmers alike. Farms built icehouses to store the ice and hold their surplus, and homeowners purchased "ice boxes" as early refrigerator systems. Having ice was considered an extravagance, but truth be told, farmers who had ice could make better butter, keep their milk from spoiling and, of course, help create ice cream. Because ice cream was so popular, the Chatham Fair's ice cream eating contest was a major attraction.

Many farms sold their raw milk to the Borden processing plant located in the Buckleyville section of Ghent. But by 1961, when a fire destroyed the plant, the industry had changed, and Borden decided not to rebuild. Many local dairies could not survive a new requirement by other processors that

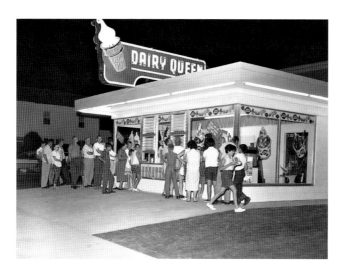

Dairy Queen in Chatham in the 1950s. *Library of Congress.*

farms install a large cold storage tank to avoid the need for daily pickups. Most local farms could not support herds of a size sufficient to justify this investment. Only twenty farms, most dairies, were left in the town by 1966, and that number had dwindled to four by 1977. The last surviving dairy farm was the Doyle farm on Route 9, which ceased operations around 2015.

The Dairy Queen in Ghent was first opened in 1963 by a couple named Harry and Helen Swift from Hudson. At first, customers would use the walk-up window to order their soft-serve cones. It wasn't until 2005 that the drive-up window was added.

LOST CAVES OF AUSTERLITZ AND BEYOND

Some of the largest and most mysterious caves in the Northeast exist in Columbia County. Merlin's Cave in Canaan, New York, discovered in 2007, is 142 feet deep. It consists of a maze of passages, a main canyon section, tight crawlspaces, large rooms, domes and a waterfall that plunges into a pool below. The cave itself is lined in blue marble.

Then there's Dragon Bone Cave, not far away from Merlin's Cave, where cave explorers detected a significant airflow in the cave from an unknown source. Inside Dragon's Bone Cave is a dome that's 211 feet in length and 65- feet deep.

Up in the dark forests, amid the dense pines and old-growth trees of the Austerlitz hills, there are some very mysterious caves as well. For centuries, it's been said that within those caves are everything from counterfeit money to a big black cat—a cougar, in fact. There have been rumors that large quantities of gold are buried in the caves beyond Fog Hill Road, and there's been talk that in 1947, the U.S. military investigated Columbia County caves as possible locations for atom bomb shelters.

The Austerlitz caves and the remote mountains into which they are set are strange. Take a walk as the sun sets in the woods in Austerlitz and into the hills, and you'll look over your shoulder more than once, feeling that perhaps someone, or something, is following. Tourists and even a few locals have found themselves lost in the thick pine forests. Some have been rescued—some not.

Oddly, the hills in Austerlitz are all named. There's East Hill, Fire Hill, West Hill, Crow Hill and Fog Hill. Crow Hill earned its name because when a flock of sheep was raided and killed, it attracted crows, who fed on the carcasses. So many crows showed up that they darkened the skies.

On Fog Hill, there was a notable character they called the "Sinatra of Spencertown." He was known by his friends as "Pop" Sweet. Pop was a fiddler, a singer and a champion square-dance caller, and his claim to fame was spotting a large black "panther" near the caves close to his home. Pop Sweet, also coined the "Fiddler of Fog Hill," had one other talent that surfaced on Groundhog Day. Pop greeted the groundhog named "Richard" each February. Bending down over the hole, Pop would take a big breath and then bellow out in his loudest roar, "Open the door, Richard!" If he received no answer from the friendly rodent, he'd ask again in an even louder voice. If he failed to appear, Pop would try his "Groundhog Song"—the one, Pop said, Richard always loved. It went like this: "Slap your hands. Slap your knees. Grab the Groundhog as you please." Just as he broke out in song, the sound of scurrying began within Richard's lair. And suddenly the groundhog appeared!

No Bottom Pond in Austerlitz is, in its own right, a force of unusual nature. Its smooth black water surface appears to be fathoms deep, with dark and daunting caves all around. In most years, by July 4, the pond goes as dry as a "salt herring," revealing the large dank holes amid the rocks. And a decent-sized stream bubbles up like Texas oil, only to be swallowed by the earth—resurfacing, some say, as far away as Queechy Lake in Canaan, New York.

Do the caves hold some dark threat? It appears so. Men have slipped inside these awaiting black mouths and are never seen again. A story out of Red Rock reports of an ox that fell into these pits and disappeared forever.

The farmer who owned the ox apparently threw a rock into No Bottom Pond after it fell, but no sound was heard. No Bottom Pond is apt to go dry overnight and may fill up and disappear at various intervals. One year, it was dry in October, and then ice fourteen inches thick was cut from it the same winter. It is about one fourth of a mile long. No one has discovered where the water comes from and where it goes, unless it is into the caves that surround the neighboring land.

In the 1950s, William McDonnell, a hunter from Brooklyn, New York, was lost for five hours in a remote section of the Austerlitz Mountains and later claimed that he was trailed by a "black panther" before he was eventually found by state police and the Columbia County deputy sheriff.

McDonnell, thirty-five and hailing from 43rd Street, Brooklyn, was the object of a widespread search when he failed to return to a car that was parked off the road on County 17, where three other members of his hunting party were waiting. The four men, all from Brooklyn, were hunting in the heavily wooded section of Mountain Ten (the former ski area) in Austerlitz. They parked their car near an open area at the former Mountain Ten ski slopes and walked into the woods at about 2:00 p.m. At sundown, three members of the party returned to the car, but McDonnell failed to appear. Two of the men walked to the nearest farm and called the state police. McDonnell, his friends said, had the keys to their car, and they had used all of their ammunition trying to signal him in the woods. A search party was organized, and in the dead of night, the woods were combed for the missing hunter. The man was eventually located on County Road 17 by the deputy sheriff.

McDonnell said that in the middle of the afternoon, he had shot a buck deer near the summit of Mountain Ten and spent some time dressing the animal. He was overtaken by darkness when he lost track of time. He had no ammunition left to signal his whereabouts. He told authorities that he left the deer and made his way out of the woods and at one time was followed by a pair of wildcats and what he described as a "black panther" that growled fiercely at him in the darkness. The deputy sheriff said that several hunters had reported seeing a large black cat in the Mountain Ten area.

Later on, Pop Sweet spotted the large cat, soon known as the "Beast of the Berkshires." Pop swore that the black critter "was holed up in No Bottom Pond Cave" in Austerlitz. Pop insisted that the beast howled at the full moon and that he found gigantic footprints leading directly to the cave.

Mysterious and foreboding, No Bottom Pond's caves have attracted thrill-seekers for centuries. Entering the area, you'll still find native pussy willow plants, wood ducks resting on the surface of the pond and ancient-looking, moss-covered stone walls where farmers kept their grazing sheep.

Centuries ago, the Austerlitz Mountains and caves were a convenient hiding place for all types of horse thieves and other miscreants, offering an easy escape route out of Massachusetts and Connecticut for those looking to evade the law. Between 1820 and 1840, local residents started to notice "queer" (a colloquial term for fake money) suddenly appearing in shops and banks. The makers of the "bogus bills" were never caught, yet some remember that the money was printed in caves near Austerlitz on the Alford, Massachusetts border. The caves were located by a resident who saw a snake crawl into a very small hole near his property.

Ambrose Woolsey and his gang of counterfeiters and horse thieves used the caves in connection with their enterprises. It is a matter of knowledge that they stole horses, took them to a cave, dyed them a different color and sold them to the U.S. Army horse buyers during the Civil War.

The horse thieves had a great way of hiding their crimes in caves. Gang members constructed a two-story barn against a rock ledge. A person entering the top floor of the barn would believe that the building contained only farm equipment and hay, but the thieves built false fronts along the interior and behind the fake walls were stalls where the thieves kept as many as forty stolen horses. This barn in Austerlitz served as one of the main "stations" that horse thieves used to transport horses stolen in Saratoga and Long Island, making stops in Austerlitz and Boston Corners in the southern portion of Columbia County. The gang member who owned the barn with the false façade was one of the few thieves ever brought to trial for the crime. The judge sentenced him to five years in prison.

In another amazing time, in 1933, local papers reported that several local boys walking the woods of Austerlitz stumbled on a strange hole. Johnnie Brooks insisted on investigating it further. He used sticks and poles to prod the spot, and when the dirt fell away, another boy, Vernon Stone, crawled through small tunnels. Despite the danger, he wiggled through small spaces until at last they discovered a large cavern. The boys told the authorities that the cave was located on the farm owned by Joseph Metal of New York City. Mr. Metal was a baker by trade. The boys said that they were stunned at what they found: "I saw a big stone in one room and I thought there was a hole, behind it. I could not move the stone, so I procured a log-chain—and with the aid of the other boys we moved it to another place and the hole was large enough for me to enter. I followed a circuitous passage sometimes erect and sometimes crawling until I found myself in a large room. There are various tunnels and passage ways, but we have not had time to thoroughly explore them." Louis Stone said that "the large rooms, had projections from the side walls that seem to have been arranged especially as hat and coat hooks." Robert Williamson Jr. found an object that was sent for geological testing. The large cavern also showed stalactites with an iridescent shine varying in size and shape, and some were transparent like ice.

If you go exploring in the woods and come across a cave, think twice before squeezing into its opening. You don't know what you'll find there.

LOST ENTERTAINMENT: THE SHOW BOAT

In the 1930s, there was a huge boat in New Lebanon, New York, sitting on dry land, nowhere near open water. It was massive, and the boat just sat there, impossible to miss. It grabbed your attention right away, like King Kong on top of the Empire State Building. The enormous vessel had all the bells and whistles of any boat you might see on the high seas. It featured an elegant promenade and a sturdy captain's bridge. Portholes like pop-out windows glared out like human eyes, and there were a few anchors flung over the sides of the ship adding to its authenticity. There was even a heavy ship mast and a ghoulish gangplank—one could imagine a disobedient crewmember being forced to walk.

In total, the boat was more than one hundred feet long and thirty feet wide. But this boat was not like any typical craft. What made this ship truly out of the ordinary was that it was equipped with a theater featuring stages at each end and cabin-like booths all around the perimeter of an enormous dance floor.

This whole faux ship in New Lebanon started with Edmund Flynn Sr. Mr. Flynn had an idea to build a dance hall just like a real cruise ship and make it a fantastic entertainment venue in his own neighborhood. Just a few miles from the Berkshire border, on the Pittsfield/Albany Road, Flynn realized that he had the perfect location to capitalize on the traffic that buzzed along the proposed location. The "Boat," as it was called, was located on what we know now as Routes 20 and 22 in New Lebanon, New York, which nearly ninety years ago was the main highway from Boston to Buffalo. Flynn decided that he would call his new night spot the Show Boat.

Flynn's hunch about a nightclub in New Lebanon, along with the fairly unenforced liquor laws in New York, proved to be the exact mix needed to

The Show Boat nightclub in New Lebanon. *Wikimedia Commons.*

attract crowds from nearby New York, as well as Pittsfield and beyond.

Big names like blues singer Ella Fitzgerald made appearances on the Show Boat's stage, along with Chick Webb, a noted musician and bandleader for a Black orchestra. Top entertainers like Tommy and Jimmy Dorsey were frequent headliners. Comedians at the Show Boat included Redd Fox, Henny Youngman and Buddy Hackett, among others who made the Show Boat a regular stop before heading on to bigger cities.

Gypsy Rose Lee and Candy Barr were popular burlesque acts. Popular singing groups including the Mills Brothers and the Ink Spots were frequently on the bill. There was a constant flow of music, amusement, dancing and fun.

The people who crowded into the club loved the headliners, but what really made the Show Boat so very popular was the uniqueness of a huge ship sitting on dry land out in the middle of the country. The pure architecture of the vessel would make any boat builder green with envy. It had glitz and glamour. The Show Boat had everything going for it until its founder died in 1935.

Directly following Flynn's death, the Show Boat was sold to Earle Roberts and his brothers. The establishment changed hands again in the mid-1940s when it was scooped up by former boxer Nicholas Pignone, who operated the club for the next twenty years.

When the club was sold a third time in 1966 to Jack Carpinello, he refocused the venue's acts on rock-and-roll and a whole lot of dancing. The visitors said that it was a good thing the Show Boat was built like a real ship because on some nights it held up to five hundred dancers on its deck.

Carpinello made a go of it until 1974, when he sold the property to two men from the Albany region, Bernie Mulligan and Fred Endres, who renamed the venue The Barrel and described it as "a melting pot for single people." Berkshire County bands that were booked included Ball of Confusion, Hot Spur and Potter Mountain Road.

Unfortunately for the newest owners, they never quite got the hang of running the spot and sold it quickly to Francis Dinova, who had plans to open the site as a dinner club.

While Dinova's plans were underway, tragedy struck the beloved night spot. One night in 1975, out of nowhere, flames sprang up from every angle and engulfed the club. Several local fire departments fought the blaze, which was reported as one of the worst fires ever in the area. Sadly, "the Boat" couldn't be saved. The famous landlocked vessel, the creation of Edmund Flynn Sr., was no more.

Part III

LOST THINGS

ADELE NELSON'S LOST ELEPHANTS OF GHENT

Adele Nelson was part of the famous circus family from Michigan that dates back to the early nineteenth century. Robert Nelson Sr. was born in London, England, in 1840. He was instrumental in forming the family's very first acrobatic troupe. After performing throughout Great Britain, they set sail for America in 1866. Robert then married Miss Emma Smart. After his marriage, they did some touring in Cuba but disbanded soon after.

Robert and his two young sons, Robert Jr. and Arthur, then performed as a Risley act. The Risley act is rather notable in the circus world because it involves an acrobat putting a person on their back, and against a support, the person balances and rolls with their feet on to other people performing acrobatic stunts. Several people can be in the bottom position, and several people fly from one set of feet to the other while performing acrobatic maneuvers.

They toured Europe several times, as well as India, and performed with a number of major circuses, including P.T. Barnum's circus from 1880 to 1882. In India in 1884, Robert Nelson Jr. married Miss Adele Burt, an equestrian and steeple-chase rider. In late 1896, Arthur Nelson married Miss Sarah Warren. After forming a tightwire act, they joined the Nelson Family of acrobats.

The Nelson Family then consisted of Robert Nelson Sr.; Robert Nelson Jr.; Alice and Elizabeth Welch (cousins); Robert Jr.'s sons, Arthur and Artie, and daughter, Adele; Sid Buttons, an apprentice; and Bill "Willie" Welch (another cousin). The family performed all kinds of acrobatics and tumbling. Sarah Nelson, Adele Nelson and Arthur Nelson also performed separate acts.

Into the early 1900s, the original family members began to fade out, retire, marry or die off. Robert Nelson Sr. died in 1916 and his wife in 1925. Robert Nelson Jr. died in July 1914 and his wife, Adele, in 1912. Robert Jr.'s son Artie later died of pneumonia. Robert Nelson Jr.'s daughter, Adele Nelson, would go on to marry elephant trainer and world traveler Lewis Reed. On January 6, 1969, the Nelson Family act was elected to the Circus Hall of Fame.

Adele Nelson's elephants on a teeterboard. *Alan Faulkner, Town of Ghent Collection.*

The Nelson Family of acrobats, often simply called the Nelsons, stunned the world. Adele was born in Mount Clemens, Michigan. Her mother was a bareback horse rider. When Adele made her circus debut at age four, she also became a bareback horse rider and learned to walk the treacherous tightrope. When Adele met world adventurer and elephant trainer Lew Reed in 1923, she fell in love, and together with her two sons (from a previous marriage), they moved to Ghent, New York, in Columbia County in 1930. There the couple purchased a 186-acre farm in Ghent, and Adele Nelson's elephant farm was born.

The family and the elephants all lived together on a farm with a big barn on Harlemville Road. Both Lew and Adele trained the three elephants, known to the family and fans as Myrtle, Tillie and Jennie. Finding venues for their act was not difficult. Throughout the 1930s and '40s, the troupe traveled from nearby Albany to Virginia and Maine, playing at everything from fairs and festivals to carnivals and small circuses. The best time for locals living in Columbia County was when the group was back home in Ghent, when the elephants would graze in the farm's fields and local kids were invited to visit.

Newspaper reporters wrote about Adele tending her elephants wearing costumes like rhinestone velvet shorts and fancy hairdos. She reportedly showed off her acrobatics for the neighborhood by doing somersaults between the elephant legs and climbing up on the great beasts' backs. The impromptu shows at Ghent were quite memorable.

There's also a story that appeared in the *Chatham Courier* about a group of hunters who were separated from their friends and wandered up onto the Nelson farm. Cresting a hill to try to locate their companions, the hunters came upon the three elephants. Much to their surprise, these were not the whitetail deer they'd hoped to find in the woods. The men "hightailed" it out of there, later recounting the discovery of the beasts to their friends.

The elephants, however, became friends to many people and animals during their time in Ghent. One day, they were called on to help haul a man's truck out of a muddy sinkhole not far from the farm. They frequently delighted neighbors on their trek home. Having been unloaded from a train car, the elephants with their trainers would walk the mile or two back to the farm. The elephants traveled quite a bit, sometimes as far as England.

In the 1960s, the *Chatham Courier* ran a piece stating that Mrs. Reed sold her farm to Mr. and Mrs. Herman Adler of Merrick, Long Island. The farm had been known as the Elephant Farm for nearly thirty years. Many would remember how the elephants, between their performing seasons, were kept in a heated barn and how Mrs. Reed's son Robert Nelson, who was with the Barnum & Bailey Circus, would train his precious pigs.

Mrs. Reed intended to retain a few acres on the farm where she would live in a trailer. Adele died in 1974 at Barnwell Nursing Home in Valatie. As an aside, several strange animal events happened on the farm. Subsequent to the sale, a TV repairman attempting to install an antenna in the attic discovered that more than one hundred various snakes had taken up residence. Another article ran in the *Chatham Courier* reporting about a woman's dog that traveled three miles to the Elephant Farm to sleep in the stable with the elephants. Even after the elephants departed, this same terrier would walk there looking for them. In 1957, a very rare pair of pure white albino deer were seen where the elephants once roamed the fields. Could the farm have some supernatural power that attracts animals? Maybe….

LOST LITERATURE: AMERICA'S FIRST BEST-SELLER ABOUT QUEECHY LAKE

According to the publishing world, one of the most popular writers of the 1850s, with maybe Harriet Beecher Stowe taking the very top spot, was Susan Warner of Canaan, New York, Columbia County. She wrote a book called *The Wide, Wide World*. The novel was first published in 1850 under her pseudonym, Elizabeth Wetherell. The book was an immediate best-seller and has seen seventy editions, with several translated into foreign languages. Warner's work was outsold only by Harriet Beecher Stowe's classic, *Uncle Tom's Cabin*. Many in the publishing world say that it was America's first best-seller. But what happened to this book?

Susan Warner loved growing up in Canaan, New York. She and her sister, Anna, spent much of the time visiting their grandfather Jason Warner at his Queechy Lake farmhouse. Susan used these cherished experiences in her novels. She even called her second book *Queechy*, and the villages she described directly resemble Canaan Center and Canaan Four Corners as they were in the mid-1800s.

Warner called the fictional town Montepoole, or what's known today as Lebanon Springs, and the lake that Susan named Deepwater is Queechy. At the time Susan was writing her book, Queechy was known as Whiting's Pond, but after the book was published, the name became so popular that there was a decision to change the lake's name permanently.

One of the more curious legends of Canaan, as told in Warner's *Queechy*, was that of a mysterious cave, "down under a mountain, a few miles to the south of this, right at the foot of a bluff some four or five hundred feet sheer down—it was known to be the resort of those creatures [rattlesnakes]; and a party of us went out…to see if we couldn't destroy the nest."

History tells us that the Warner family came to Canaan in 1764, just a few years after the first settlers, and that the head of the family, William, built a tavern near the Canaan Center Presbyterian Church. William's nine sons fought together under Colonel William Whiting during the Revolutionary War. The second son, Henry Whiting Warner (1787–1875), went to Union College in Schenectady and became a successful lawyer. In 1817, he married a stunning socialite, Miss Anna Barrett. They had two daughters; Susan was born on July 11, 1819, in New York City.

After a visit to West Point, William fell in love with the island near the east shore of the Hudson called Constitution Island. The family moved there and spent the rest of their lives on the island. Susan and

Vintage *Queechy* book cover. *Author's photo.*

Anna's mother died when they were very small, and the girls were raised by their Aunt Fanny. It was Aunt Fanny who encouraged Susan's writing when money became tight. Both Susan and Anna together wrote more than seventy books. The sisters also wrote a popular hymn called "Say and Seal" in 1859, and Anna wrote "Jesus Loves Me," which is now known worldwide.

Susan Warner's ancestors were among the early New England settlers in the colonies, dating back to the Pilgrim days and beyond. John Alden and Pricilla Mullins, who came over on the *Mayflower*, and Colonel William Whiting, who took part in the battle at Saratoga during the Revolution, were some of her relatives. Puritan blood ran through Susan Warner's veins. She came from pious people, yet two of her relatives who lived in the infamous town of Salem, Massachusetts, were publicly condemned during the witch trials.

Ms. Warner's great-grandmother Rebecca Lupton had nine sons, all six feet in height; each of them followed their father into the Continental army, and the youngest played the fife in the ranks until he was old enough to fight. A story was told in the family that Grandmother Lupton once sent out her very best feather pillow to a party that was determined to tar and feather a Tory spy.

Jason Warner, Susan's grandfather, was also a soldier of the Revolution. He was tall at six feet, two inches, and he bathed in the waterfall on the farm in Canaan. A great worshiper of the country he served, he named one of his sons George Washington.

Susan's uncle was a professor at West Point from 1822 to 1832, and as a result, he developed a passion for religion and served the military faithfully.

Susan was born on July 11, 1819, in New York City. Her family was wealthy on her mother's side. Her mother was a socialite, and her father was a prominent lawyer. They lived in an elegant townhouse at St. Mark's Place. The family employed a battalion of servants to clean and cook and care for Susan and her sister, Anna. Out in front of their elegant home sat a beautiful carriage. The house was equipped with a greenhouse and many fine furnishings. As was the custom of socially prominent families in New York, Susan studied with tutors and lived a luxurious life. She excelled at her Italian lessons, and she adored painting and doing her lacework. While the city was her home, she spent her summers in the country at her grandfather's farmhouse in Canaan.

If you asked anyone to describe Susan, they'd say that she was a very vivacious child who was delicate and kind and loved to read. In fact, Susan read all types of books. One summer day, a trip was planned to see the

Shakers at Mount Lebanon, but Susan protested and begged to be left at the farm to read her books. She said that she'd prefer to read Cowper than to "see all the Shakers in the world!"

Susan clearly preferred her imagination to activities. She loved to make up "talk stories," which she had her friends recite like plays. When she turned twelve, Susan started writing in a journal.

When Susan's mother died, things changed for her dramatically. At a time when she needed comfort from her only remaining parent, she found none in her father, who buried himself in financial speculations that ultimately failed during the crash of 1837,

Susan Warner's author portrait. *Library of Congress.*

leaving him and the children without one red cent! While visiting his brother, Thomas, a chaplain at West Point, Henry Warner, now a widower with two young girls, was looking for a summer house.

It seems that one of Mr. Warner's financial speculations ended in the purchase of Constitution Island, a spit of land just off the shore from West Point on the opposite shore of the Hudson River. When Warner realized that he had no money, he sold off his beautiful New York home and moved his girls to the strange island in the river. The deserted island had an old barracks, which Henry thought might be ideal for his family. When he bought the island, he added an eight-room Victorian wing with high ceilings onto the Revolutionary War structure. He relied on the kindness of the girls' Aunt Fanny to help with the household. Aunt Fanny cared for Susan and Anna, and it was Fanny who ultimately became a mother to the two young girls for the duration of their lives.

For a young woman of the time, Susan was unusually tall. She was nearly six feet tall and had a very long neck. Most people who knew her said that she was quite charming and loving, although she was awfully serious. She was prone to melancholy, which caused her to have "spells" of weeping and dark moods. She clung to her religious beliefs and was gravely affected by death, and later, Susan's characters would hold some of the same deeply emotional traits.

By the spring of 1848, Susan had begun writing her very first and later her most famous novel. At the suggestion of her aunt, she put away her childhood and began her life as a true writer. Her sister, Anna, in a biography she would later write about her sister, wrote of how *The Wide, Wide World* began. She said that one night, as they were casually finishing dinner and doing the dishes, her aunt leaned over toward Susan and almost whispered in her ear like a muse, "You could probably write a story to sell if you want to." It wasn't that far-fetched, given that Susan's father, Henry W. Warner, had already written a few books about law. Susan, despite her moodiness as a teenager, had a fighting spirit and the kind of determination needed to finish a volume of her own. Her jumping-off point came from her feelings about the death of her mother. She believed that she could write about a theme of a "desolate child tossed out upon the world," and she began that very night.

Using her pen name, Elizabeth Wetherell, she completed the book in one short year, and by the summer of 1849, *The Wide, Wide World* was ready for all the world to see. Susan was just turning thirty-five.

By this time, money was very tight, and the family were suffering. Susan's father had to sell off their possessions, including the family's furniture. Getting Susan's book published was critical, but it wouldn't prove to be easy. Publishers refused her almost completely. The leading book publishing firms in New York wrote back calling the book "fudge." In the summer of 1850, the book was taken to George Putnam, who had his mother, Catherine, read it. She was quoted as saying to him, "Son, if you never publish another book, publish this." And so he did.

At first, the book sold slowly. But then *The Wide, Wide World* flew off the shelves. In one short year, the book sold more than 1,400 copies, and a new edition was ordered. By the end of 1852, the book was in its fourteenth edition.

During this period, it seems that domestic life was a common focus of popular novels. These novels were extremely popular in middle-class American homes, and sales soared, making the publishers ecstatic. Unfortunately, authors of other books in the 1850s suffered. The era was later coined by Frederick Lewis Pattee as the "Feminine Fifties" because so many women authored these books. Nathaniel Hawthorne was not so pleased with the rise of female authors. He was quoted as saying, "America is now wholly given over to a much-damned mob of scribbling women and I should have no chance of success while the public taste is occupied with such trash." Susan's book would eventually go on to sell 1 million copies.

Taking a chance, during November and December 1850 and even before her first novel was published, Susan had an idea for a second book she would call *Queechy*. She sketched out the storyline as she had done as a child, and by early 1851, she'd finished the first draft.

By the winter of 1851–52, both she and her sister, Anna, were busily writing books they hoped would be published in the spring. Anna had written a book called *Dollars and Cents*, which was to follow Susan's final draft of *Queechy*. As luck would have it, they both were published in April 1852. On April 21, 1851, George P. Putnam published *Queechy*. The first edition was in two volumes and cost $1.75. The first volume was bursting with 410 pages, and the second volume was not much slimmer at 396 pages. The book was "stereotyped" by Ballin & Brothers, which had a shop downtown at William Street in New York City. Later copies in the twentieth century featured a picture of a red-haired girl on the cover. In all, *Queechy* was reprinted thirty-four times. Susan wrote in her journal that Putnam ordered five thousand copies on the first run of the book, which was among one of the largest first orders ever produced in his store. Seven editions would eventually be published in England in 1853. The British Museum catalogue listed the book. A British clipper ship was named *Freda* in honor of the main character of *Queechy*.

As was the custom, the sisters took pen names. Susan's was "Elizabeth Wetherell," and Anna took "Amy Lothrop." The inspiration for the new names came from the maiden names of their great-grandmother.

It wouldn't take long for Susan's book to earn enough money to let them pay back money they had borrowed. The sisters could even afford riding lessons, a piano and a few luxuries like black silk dresses. In the summer of that year, they bought back the family's furniture, which had been sold to the Roosevelts. Although they received payment for their books, the two sisters didn't earn as much as they should have. As women, they were swindled out of proceeds when some of their books were purchased outright for cash while few laws were in place, internationally, to protect them. When their books were sold in England, they received no payments at all. Tens of thousands of copies of *Queechy* were sold at an English railway station without Susan receiving a single dollar.

After 1852, Susan and Anna collaborated, writing everything from short stories to newspaper and magazine articles. They even attempted to publish a magazine of their own. During the Civil War, the two sisters produced a newspaper called the *Little American*. They worked night and day and were employed to correct compositions and prepare Sunday school lessons. They even sold vegetables to earn money.

Susan would go on to write an astonishing twenty novels after *Queechy*, but none of them compared to her first two. In the 1870s, Susan wrote three new stories that sold reasonably well. Her longtime publisher, George

Putnam, remarked that Miss Warner "had retained her reading public for a longer term of years than was the case possibly with any other American writer of fiction." In fact, Susan Warner's books were popular right up to the beginning of World War I, as they continued to be the choice of fiction for women who preferred sentimental stories.

When Susan died on March 17, 1885, she was buried at the West Point Cemetery at the request of the cadets. Apparently, they had held a Sunday afternoon Bible class at their home on Constitution Island many years prior. The cadets were eternally grateful. Anna Warner, the last of her family, had been repeatedly offered huge sums of money for the purchase of Constitution Island. The would-be buyers, however, had planned manufacturing or recreation, and Anna refused. She felt that the island should belong only to the government. In 1908, Anna sold the island to the philanthropist Margaret Olivia Sage for $175,000. Mrs. Russell Sage, in a letter to President Theodore Roosevelt, bequeathed the land to West Point, with the provision that Miss Warner should keep her home there during her lifetime.

Paying homage to her older sister, in 1910 Anna published *The Life and Letters of Susan Warner*. The media marveled at how the volume was so lovingly edited by Susan's younger sister. "Few writers have had biographers so minutely careful as to every word written, or so worshipful of their subject as this one."

When Anna died in 1915, she, too, was buried at West Point and, like her sister, with full military honors. The Warner sisters are probably the only civilian women buried at the West Point Cemetery. Susan's headstone reads that she was the author of *The Wide, Wide World*.

It is said that Susan's most popular novels told the same basic story with only a few variations. The books focused on a young girl who had lived a life of luxury as a child and then suddenly was forced into poverty because of a financial fall. Yet the story of *Queechy* can be said to follow Susan's life more closely.

The lake of Canaan is easy to recognize as "Deepwater Lake," once known as "Whiting's Pond," and the farmhouse as "Queechy Run." "Rattlesnake Run" might be identified as what is known as Perry's Peak, and many other places mentioned in the novel might ring a bell or two if you're familiar with this portion of Columbia County. "Montepoole" is the Native American name given to the healing springs of Lebanon Mountain, once a thriving health resort in the 1840s. The book's characters were clearly based on real people Susan once knew, including Susan's Aunt Fanny and her grandfather.

Not to put too fine a point on Susan Warner's books, but her work was read by such notables as Vincent van Gogh, Elizabeth Barrett Browning, Rudyard Kipling, Mrs. George Bancroft and the daughter of Charles Darwin. "Miss Darwin's niece remembered that the book was read aloud to them with all of the religion left out and all the good country food left in," according to the *Chatham Courier* in 1966.

What's possibly even more fascinating are the efforts on the part of West Point to preserve and reconstruct the Warner house as it was on Constitution Island. The island has been the home of the Nochpeem Tribe of Native Americans, early Dutch settlers, American Revolutionary War soldiers and, of course, the Warner family. It was a site of respite for many West Point cadets, who rowed across the Hudson River. Coincidentally, the cadets' landing place is exactly at the same spot where the Great Chain was anchored in 1778, protecting the Hudson River and the independence of the United States from the British attack.

After remaining in storage for nearly twelve years while the Warner house was being restored, the original artifacts, personal effects and belongings of the Warner family were returned to Constitution Island for the 2024 season.

THE LOST GHOST OF MARY CHASE HAUNTS OLD CHATHAM

Not with vain longings would I have ye stand…In my loved haunts
and gaze around with pain.
—*Mary Chase*

About two miles outside the town of Old Chatham sits the Old Chase House. Mary Chase, a Quaker and poetess, was born there on August 12, 1822, just about two hundred years ago. At the time of Mary's birth, what we know as Old Chatham was actually called Chatham Four Corners. It seems that the residents of Old Chatham refused to allow a railroad center to be built in the town square. The train center was never built, leaving Old Chatham to remain the sleepy little out-of-the-way place it still is.

Mary and her parents were Quakers. Although not formally educated, Mary's mother was a lover of nature, and Mary lived an idyllic life with her family, wandering among the wonderful natural beauty and hills of

Old Chatham, eating wild apples and strawberries, listening to the sweet sounds of songbirds and taking in the bucolic countryside. Mary, like many poets (Edna St. Vincent Millay comes to mind), found that her natural surroundings inspired her writing. She grew up on the family farm, with its sweeping views of the distant Catskill Mountains. There her father established a small school.

By 1843, at age twenty-one, Mary had entered the Albany Female Academy, where, after a year, she graduated with honors and received a gold medal for composition. She stayed in Albany with relatives and edited a magazine called the *Monthly Rose*. At that time, she was awarded two more prizes for her poems and, in 1846, another for her essay on flowers, which, she found early on, was her passion. Although it was rare for young women at the time, Mary left her home to teach composition at the Brooklyn Female Academy in New York City. During her very first winter there, she became gravely ill. Her lungs had failed her, and she was sent back to Old Chatham weak and tired.

Though still unsteady from her illness, she began to teach at her father's small school. Mary taught all day and found herself nursing invalids by night, rarely sleeping long. At one point, Mary called in a young doctor to help a fellow teacher who was experiencing inflammation of the lungs. According to a local account, "the doctor bled him at once, while Mary stood by with the dish 'like the fish in Cock Robin, to catch his blood.'"

Mary was a generous soul and took to visiting the community of Quakers in Rayville, a small community just north of Old Chatham, bringing little gifts. She sometimes helped her Aunt Isabel carry bundles of dried herbs to the village store in Chatham to exchange them for home goods and medicine.

Mary's early poetry was considered quite brilliant. She wrote her poem "The Three Days' French Revolution" when she was only eight years old. Her teacher deemed it "extraordinary and with a pardonable zeal" sent it to the city newspaper, where it was published in the "poet's corner."

In the spring of 1851, she returned to the Brooklyn Academy to fill a faculty position, but within a short time, she was bored and miserable and longed for the hills and countryside of her home in Columbia County. At a time in her life when she was longing for a change, she fell in love with a young man at the academy. Excited to have her family meet her new beau, she invited him to come home to the farm with her for the holidays and share her poetry with him in all the places she adored, as well as share the deep woods, the aroma of lilacs in spring and the crisp night air. Sadly, nowhere does it say that the young man ever accompanied her to her beloved home.

Mary returned to the place she loved, Old Chatham. She loved the fields and meadows, the orchards and trees. She committed herself to nature in her poetry, and when she died of tuberculosis on November 3, 1852, at the young age of thirty, she asked to be buried under the apple tree on the farm.

Since Mary Chase's passing, the house where she lived and wrote her poetry in Old Chatham has generated some strange stories. In 1920, the house, then abandoned, was purchased by a man named H.A. von Behr. He was a well-regarded New York City portrait and commercial photographer. Von Behr was the not the first to report that the former home of Mary Chase was inhabited by her spirit. He would eventually go on to put his paranormal experiences in a book called *Ghosts in Residence.*

When Von Behr purchased the house, it was still called the Old Chase House after Mary's family, who built it in 1790. According to Von Behr, the ghost of Mary Chase roamed the house freely. Apparently, Von Behr said that Mary felt so comfortable on her visits that she brought with her a variety of other spirits from the other side. It seems that the Chase home that Von Behr purchased was fairly inexpensive. It was only after witnessing the appearance of Mary's apparition that Von Behr realized why the home was listed at such a bargain price. Von Behr soon found out that the previous owners could not bear to stay in the home due to the persistent hauntings and disturbances. Presences made themselves known quite frequently. Things moved in the oddest of ways. Doors closed and opened by themselves. Rather than run, Von Behr and his family did the opposite: they stayed in the house and embraced the ghosts, despite one particular episode when Von Behr and his dog witnessed a strange mist rising from Mary's nearby grave, which he had repaired and restored. He said he watched in awe as the mist wafted past them and rose into the night sky. It is said that Von Behr had an affectionate relationship with his "unquiet" house.

In the book called *Mary M. Chase and Her Writings*, written by Henry Fowler in 1855, a few clues are written to possibly explain Mary Chase's reappearance on the Old Chatham family farm. Her brother, Thurston, is quoted as having said, "Her calm independence and earnestness of manner, united with her chastened language, told that there was a secret influence awakening her soul to the clearest perceptions of the beauties of the unseen as well as the visible world."

In addition to her brother's observations of her ability to transcend the world of the living and the dead, Mary's father once said, "Death to her was the fulfillment of life, not its failure." Mary had her own particular view of life and death. She wrote this verse:

It is not new, it is not strange,
his sudden, mystic, mighty change; To gain our life, not lose our life; Is the
grand end of all this strife.

Whether Mary Chase still walks the fields of flowers at the Old Chase House in Columbia County is still a mystery. But one fact remains unchanged. The site where Mary is buried is marked simply, "Mary's Grave." It's under an old oak tree that she loved to climb deep in the woods at her beloved farm.

THE LOST LOVES OF EDNA ST. VINCENT MILLAY AND MARTIN VAN BUREN

Edna St. Vincent Millay, the Pulitzer Prize–winning poet, lived in a modest farmhouse she called Steepletop, at the top of East Hill Road in Austerlitz with her husband, Eugen Boissevain. She lived in Austerlitz, New York, in Columbia County for about thirty years starting in late 1926 until her death in 1950. She was a complex and highly accomplished woman, breaking more glass ceilings for women than any of us can count.

Millay was a native of Rockland, Maine. She was best known for her poem "Renascence." In 1923, she was awarded the Pulitzer Prize for her "The Ballad of the Harp Weaver." She told friends that she moved to Austerlitz to have a quiet place to write.

To the world's great surprise, she married a much older man, Eugen Boissevain, a Dutch importer, the same year she moved to Columbia County. Boissevain dutifully gave up his business to serve wife as a secretary and to act as her buffer against the public so that she could write without distraction.

Edna found success early in life. As with other poets of the time, Millay first saw her poems in print in the "club" pages of the juvenile magazine *St. Nichols*. She was still a student, at the age of nineteen, when her first major poem, "Renascence," was published in 1912.

In her twenties, she became a well-known figure in New York's avant-garde Greenwich Village arts scene. Millay was not linear in her work. She was often restless and wrote in fits and starts, working hard, scrawling her poems in notebooks, long-hand, and then doing nothing for weeks. Among her many best-remembered works is "There Are No Islands Any More," which was published at the outset of World War II. She wrote *Collected Sonnets*, published in 1941, and *Collected Lyrics* in 1944.

There is possibly a misconception that the Pulitzer Prize–winning poet was a cold and unemotional person who rarely created lasting friendships. Rumors often swirled of her demanding self, and it's well known that she engaged in extramarital love affairs. Millay even wrote of an imaginary lover in her diary as a child. But when she met George Dillon, Edna changed her ways and possibly fell in love, genuinely, for the first time.

Although this information goes unpublished in most of the books about the poet's life, edited out to purify her memory, Edna St. Vincent Millay had a twenty-year extramarital relationship with poet George Dillon. Her sister, Norma, it's been reported, burned her love letters.

In Mary Oliver's book, *Blue Pastures*, the author talks openly about a visit she had with Millay's sister, Norma, who pleaded with her not to let the secret of Millay and Dillon "out." Although Millay had many affairs, Norma Millay said that this one was different because it wouldn't "die out."

Love Is Not All is a collection of fifty-two sonnets written by Edna St. Vincent Millay. The collection was first published in the sonnet sequence *Fatal Interview* in 1931. Despite a raging economic depression, it took just a few short months for the book sales to reach fifty thousand copies. The collection is a direct link to Dillon, navigating the rise and fall of the love affair.

Millay first met the very attractive George Dillon by accident on November 2, during one of during her reading tours promoting a new volume of *The Buck in the Snow*, at the University of Chicago in 1928. Despite their age difference, she was thirty-six and he was just twenty-one, Millay pursued him.

After Millay's reading, Dillon attended a small reception in her honor at the home of her friend the poet Gladys Campbell, who had accompanied Dillon that night. She pushed him in front of her guests and insisted that he recite some of his latest poems from his new volume, *Boy in the Wind*.

By the very next day, after a brief meeting at the party, Millay had invited him to meet her. It was the start of a relationship that would change the trajectory of Dillon's personal and professional life, and the same would be true for Millay.

Reportedly, Edna didn't keep her new tryst to herself and spilled the news first to her loyal husband, Boissevain. As the whole affair heated up, the young, inexperienced Dillon tried to cut it off early on, but Millay wouldn't have it. This constant push and pull showed up intensely in Millay's work. Her "connection" with Dillon stretched itself out from Chicago to New York City, to Paris and then and all the way to Austerlitz, New York. Millay would bring Dillon to Steepletop, sometimes with Eugen Boissevain in the next room.

While in Paris, Boissevain and Millay entered into a trial marital separation. Although they would continue to live together in Austerlitz, she would have the freedom to pursue a relationship with Dillon. Millay was the pursuer and wrote volumes of letters and poems to Dillon in those first torrid months. While the two were staying in Paris, Boissevain wrote, "Settle down quietly, Edna, take a place for a year or come back here with him, do what you like."

The intensity of his passion for Millay, who remained quite devoted to her husband, confused and frustrated Dillon. Millay had altered his mind and invaded his heart and body, and in her absence, Dillon's passion played out in his poetry: "I think you are closer to me than anything—Not as a dream alone, but as a part: I feel your breast beat through me like a wing, I feel your hands immediate on my heart. You are the noose of sleep pulled slowly tight; You are the pulsing nerve in tooth and toe; You are the sweat upon me in the night; You are the engine urging me to go."

Founder and editor of *Poetry* magazine Harriet Monroe became one of Dillon's most devoted advocates. She even made him an associate editor of the magazine. His second volume, *The Flowering Stone* (1932), published when he was just twenty-five years old, made him one of the youngest poets ever to win the Pulitzer Prize. Yet even after this success, he faded almost completely out of the literary scene. He managed to turn to translating the work of other poets into lucrative work, and eventually he took over Monroe's place at *Poetry* after her sudden death in 1936. After this explosion onto the poetry scene as a poet, Dillon's flowering stone had finally dried up.

Although Millay was intent on helping Dillon with his career, he never produced another book of poetry. Dillon remained a bachelor until his death in 1968.

Millay eventually went back to Austerlitz, back to Boissevain, back to her security in Columbia County and back to her hilltop retreat, Steepletop. She lived on East Hill Road until her tragic death in 1950. Millay's ashes are interred next to her husband on the Steepletop property.

Martin Van Buren was the eighth president of the United States. Some could say that Van Buren's first love was politics, yet he married Hannah Hoes, a girl from his hometown of Kinderhook, New York, in Columbia County. Her and Martin's ancestors were from Holland, and Dutch was her first language. She was a shy, blue-eyed, blond-haired girl whom Martin always called "Jannetje," a Dutch form of Hannah. Sadly, Hannah succumbed to tuberculosis one month after her thirty-sixth birthday, when their children were small. Apparently, Hannah was slow to recover from the birth of her fifth child in January 1817. By the following winter, her health was failing. In fact, her health had begun to decline soon after Martin moved the family to Albany in 1817. By September 1818, she was pregnant, but she was no longer able to leave the house. She was confined mainly to her bed and able to see her children only for a few minutes at a time. That winter, shortly after giving birth to Smith Thompson, their fourth surviving son, she died. Out of respect for her memory, Van Buren never mentioned her last days. In fact, he never mentioned her death at all.

After Hannah Van Buren died in Albany on February 5, 1819, her service was held at the Dutch Reformed Church in Kinderhook, with interment in the church cemetery. At Hannah's request, the custom of providing scarves for the pallbearers to wear at the funeral was abandoned, and the money set aside to pay for them was used to feed the poor. Hannah Van Buren died eighteen years before her husband was sworn in as president. She would never serve as first lady.

After his young wife's death, Martin Van Buren became something of a "dandy." In the words of Davy Crockett, "He struts and swaggers like a crow in a gutter." Van Buren didn't remarry, and he didn't acquire his first daughter-in-law until many years later when his eldest son, Abraham, married a southern girl named Sarah Angelica Singleton, who was the cousin of First Lady Dolley Todd Madison, wife of James Madison. Sarah was a woman who loved all things French and even changed her name to "Angelica."

In March 1838, Mrs. Madison brought Angelica and her sisters to a private White House dinner hosted by the widower, President Martin Van Buren. The president's four unmarried adult sons were seated around the table. The stage seemed to be set for matchmaking.

In the first few minutes of the dinner, it became quite apparent that Angelica was attracted to the president's son Abraham, a dashing West Point graduate who wore a sash and a sword. The sparks between them were romantically charged enough to deliver Angelica and Abraham to the altar just eight months later.

As was the custom, the newlyweds moved directly into the White House with the bachelor president. Angelica promptly installed herself as a most elegant White House hostess. Van Buren couldn't have been more delighted. Yet it wasn't long before rumors began to fly regarding the nature of the relationship between Martin and Angelica as she graduated from a mere hostess to become her father-in-law's first lady. The move was quite unusual.

Angelica Van Buren portrait. *Library of Congress.*

Never before had the White House witnessed such a strange arrangement. Despite its potential impropriety in Washington's social circles, Martin Van Buren always escorted Angelica on his arm to all formal private dinners at the White House and made it clear that her rank and status took precedence over any other women in attendance at any White House gathering.

Angelica Singleton was born in 1818 and was, unofficially, First Lady no. 8. Angelica's style and beauty caused her to become something of a minor celebrity. Newspaper articles pointed to her beauty, and the fact that she was *not* the president's wife was always underscored. In the White House portrait gallery, her portrait sat next to a quaint, smaller portrait of original Mrs. Martin Van Buren, which also hung near the portrait of Dolley Madison. The beautiful Angelica Singleton's elaborate portrait was painted by Henry Inman in about 1842. Inman also painted a portrait of Martin Van Buren. It's been said that even when Pat Nixon, the former first lady, refurbished the Red Room in the White House, she kept Angelica's portrait above the mantel.

When Angelica and Abraham left the White House for Lindenwald in Kinderhook, New York, Angelica used what she had witnessed firsthand regarding the running of a large household during her upbringing to help her father-in-law run his estate in Kinderhook. Since serving as the main hostess at the White House, she was more than prepared to assume the management of a large mansion, and her fine private school education was the perfect training ground for entertaining. Still, at just twenty-four years old, Angelica leaned on her mother, Rebecca, to advise her on provisions for the estate. In 1840, she wrote to her mother, "First I want you to send me a list of supplies such as you usually send to Charleston in the Fall when the house is out of everything—I want it as a guide in ordering groceries, for Lindenwald and I have but an imperfect idea of the quantities of sugar, etc. especially for six month's consumption with a regular family."

Once Angelica arrived at Lindenwald in 1841, she assumed most of the duties of the mistress of the house in the family's first years. Like all mistresses of large households, she directed a staff of servants but performed some of the household work herself as well. It seems that Angelica was comfortable serving as Martin Van Buren's first lady once again.

With the White House rumors circling Angelica's strange role as first lady behind them, the family might have simply enjoyed their Lindenwald family experience without stress and strain, but that wasn't to be the case. Strangely, Martin Van Buren successfully stirred up another romantic skirmish with his second son, John. Although Martin Van Buren had strong ties with his son John and the two were extremely close, almost best friends, a woman nearly separated them forever.

Fanny Elssler was one of the first ballerinas to perform in the United States. In 1835, she starred in the Paris Opera Ballet. Five years later, she sailed to America. During the voyage, an intruder entered her cabin, seeking to rob her of her jewels. With no weapon at her disposal, Fanny used the only thing she knew and turned a pirouette so strong that she landed her foot on the man with such force she knocked him unconscious. The papers reported that the man later died of his injuries.

Once in America, she went straight to Washington, wishing to meet the famous widowed president Martin Van Buren. Fanny performed for Martin and for the fellows in Congress as a special debut. With Fanny directing all of her attention to Martin, he was having the time of his life and became the envy of his colleagues. That was, until his son John showed up. Introducing John to Fanny, Martin sadly found that he was no match for John's charm and youth. In a short time, John gained Fanny's affection and Martin was sent to the sidelines.

As John's relationship heated up with Fanny, his relationship with his father became cooler and cooler. Finally, the two stopped speaking altogether. When Fanny left on tour, John traipsed obediently after her. As the days wore on, John, though earlier smitten with Fanny at first, grew bored and tired of the road, shows and waiting for his love, and he returned to Washington. Luckily for John, Martin was neither hurt nor angry about the situation, and the two continued their close relationship.

Only one other time, while living at Lindenwald, did Martin Van Buren romantically pine away for a beautiful young lady. It was said that there was a tree, under which Martin Van Buren's horse was tethered, where a bald spot was worn into the grass while Martin so often conversed with a young local woman. He was an attendant at the Reformed Church but not a communicant. The woman told Van Buren that as a condition of their marriage, he must convert to a communicant of the church. Alas, he refused the request, and in turn, the lady refused his proposal of marriage. Van Buren remained a widower and bachelor, according to the *Albany Times Union* of July 3, 1920.

It appears that Martin Van Buren loved being the center of attention. He loved to strut around. He loved beautiful women, and like many country gentlemen farmers in Columbia County, he loved great horses, a good cigar and plenty of socializing. But one of the most hidden loves of Martin Van Buren seems to have been his bathtub.

In 1841, Martin Van Buren bought the old Van Ness House in Kinderhook and named it Lindenwald. He instantly started renovating, expanding and improving the old Dutch home. Some of the changes he made to the house were grand. He installed spacious balconies, grand lawns and beautiful fireplaces. But it wasn't until Martin installed a bathtub that the neighborhood took notice. The people of Kinderhook gathered, they gossiped and they laughed. Martin Van Buren had installed a bathtub.

Lindenwald, an original painting by Allison Marchese.

They found that to be simply unheard of and ridiculous. The fact was that no one in Columbia County, despite their wealth, had a bathtub. Most people of that time considered bathtubs simply pretentious and unhealthy. Bathtubs were for women. Locals believed that a bathtub made people "soft and decadent."

Martin's friends who heard about the bathtub were concerned about his mental state and even consulted the local physician. They explained to Martin that the doctors said that baths were dangerous! Bathing removed perspiration, important for regulating a body's temperature. Baths left the skin unprotected by removing an outer layer. Baths could even be fatal in winter. One could catch pneumonia! Martin just laughed. He explained to his friends that he'd been bathing for years, and he was still alive. Asked if he bathed every day, Martin shocked his friends by saying yes. When neighbors noticed that not only did Martin Van Buren *not die* from taking baths, but rather he even started looking more and more healthy, they did something outrageous: they installed bathtubs too. More and more people of Kinderhook used their tubs, dunking their children and finding their health improving. Within a half century, bathtubs in houses became essential.

LOST SPECIES: DINOSAURS OF CHURCHTOWN

The World's Fair of 1964 took place at Flushing Meadows Corona Park, in Queens, New York. The theme encompassed all things futuristic, and the fantastic notion of a "Space Age" was introduced. However, not all of the exhibitions were forward-thinking. The Sinclair Oil Company sponsored a wildly creative exhibit called "Dinoland," which featured life-size replicas of nine enormous dinosaurs, including a seventy-foot-long version of the Sinclair Oil Corporation's signature mascot, the *Brontosaurus*.

The sign for the attraction read, "The Exciting World of Dinosaurs shown in their natural prehistoric environment in a fascinating educational exhibit." The dinosaurs were created by Louis Paul Jonas (1894–1971) in his workshop in Churchtown, New York, in Columbia County.

Churchtown is a hamlet located about three miles from the town of Claverack, New York, in Columbia County. Among Churchtown's first inhabitants were Jacob Hagadorn, Nicholas Roat, Jonas Roshman (Rossman) and Joseph Hauser (Houser). Uldrich Sours was also one of the local landowners and surprisingly lived to be 105 years old.

In the early days, the hamlet was quite small, with just a schoolhouse owned and operated by the church, a store and several pubs or "publick houses." The hamlet also had a wagon repair shop, critical to life back in those early days; a gristmill; a sawmill; and a mill for making plaster. A lovely stream surrounded the hamlet, and the land mostly belonged to farmers. In

1853, a post office was created, and deliveries of mail came in from Hudson on a weekly basis.

Over time, Churchtown has remained a simple yet beautiful little out-of-the-way place with some lovely churches, dairy farms, a fire department and so on. That is, until Louis Paul Jonas arrived.

In the 1960s, Louis Paul Jonas was hired for an astounding $1 million contract to design exact replicas of the nine fiberglass dinosaurs to inhabit the new "Dinoland" at the World's Fair. Jonas was well known for his museum dinosaurs, including the exhibits at the Yale Peabody Museum of Natural History in New Haven, Connecticut, and the Berkshire Museum in Pittsfield, Massachusetts.

Jonas and his wife, Virginia, lived in Hillsdale, New York, with their three daughters, Debbie, Lisa and Robin, and his son, Paul. The family moved from Mahopac, New York, to Columbia County. In Mahopac, Jonas had leased an old railroad station from the New York Central for use as a studio. He was forced to move from the station because the scope of his work grew too large and the station was entirely too small for what was coming next.

It was clear that Jonas enjoyed working on big projects. Earlier in his career, Mr. Jonas and his associates in 1950 built the largest diorama in the world at Caracas, the biggest ever constructed for use at a museum.

Jonas was born in Budapest, Hungary, in 1894. He was the third son of a Hungarian mail carrier. His older brothers, Colman and Guy, had already taken up the art of taxidermy in Hungary and moved to America. By 1908, the two brothers had earned enough money to open their own business, and Jonas Brothers Taxidermy was born. Louis Paul moved to the United States to join his two brothers in the taxidermy business they had set up in Denver, Colorado. He was just fourteen years old, yet Louis had a talent for sculpting anatomy and an amazing ability to reproduce wild animals in clay and bronze.

After a few years with his brothers, he moved to New York City and became an apprentice to Carl Akeley, a noted field naturalist, taxidermist and animal sculptor at the American Museum of Natural History. It was with Akeley that Louis learned his art as a master sculptor of wildlife both big and small.

By 1947, Mr. Jonas had found a 120-acre farm on an expansive hill on Miller Road in Churchtown, New York, in Columbia County, where he located the new Jonas Studio. Over a two-year period, Jonas Studio worked to design and create the fantastic prehistoric beasts for the museums, schools,

The dinosaurs of Churchtown. *Wikimedia Commons.*

collectors and, of course, the bigger-than-life dinos for the World's Fair. Remarkably, two of Jonas's dinosaurs were even mechanized: the nineteen-foot-tall *Tyrannosaurus rex* and the immense *Brontosaurus*, which produced a stunning and sometimes frightening effect. Although they were nestled up a dirt road in a remote location, visitors from as far away as Japan made the trek to see the fiberglass dinosaurs on the studio's farm in Churchtown.

Creating dinosaurs was no easy task. The Jonas Studio had to build large special buildings to house the fabricated animals. When it came to building the exact replicas, Louis went to an expert and hired the famed paleontologists Barnum Brown and Edwin Colbert of the American Museum of Natural History to help. He also received assistance from John Ostrom of the Peabody to ensure the accuracy of his creations.

The mammoth lifelike dinosaurs included a seventy-two-foot-long *Brontosaurus*, the "Great Thunder Lizard," the largest land creature known to have existed. Reassembled bones and other material obtained from all available paleontological data made it possible for Jonas to build the physical structures. Louis also applied fifteen thousand pounds of clay to heavy wooden armature frames with steel, wire and cloth used to form the dinosaurs. After the initial structure was in place, Louis would then go to work meticulously molding the exterior to look as lifelike as possible. When done, the animal would weigh seven thousand pounds.

Jonas once confessed to a New York reporter that one of the downsides of making these magical beasts was that he dreamed of them at night. "They're always chasing me," he said. "At first, I could out run 'em without any trouble. Now, every night, they come closer to catching me."

Once the dinosaurs were completed, Louis and his team took on the daunting task of getting the animals to New York for the famous fair. It was decided by the sponsors that the transport from Hudson to New York City was to take place in full view of the public. Sinclair Oil wanted maximum publicity, so the company ran ads in the newspapers warning the public not to panic if they were to see these great beasts.

The ads read: "Giant Dinosaurs Seen on the Hudson Headed for the City. Don't worry—They're Friendly. Sinclair Dinosaurs On Way to Sinclair

World's Fair Exhibit." "Tomorrow's the Day!" the ad broadcast. "Millions of people in skyscrapers, on commuter trains and highways along the Hudson, on ships and planes, on docks and bridges will see a sight to amaze even sophisticated New Yorkers as nine Dinosaurs sail majestically around Manhattan Island." They even published a timetable regarding when the dinos would be visible. "Watch the River," the ad commanded. "You will see the 70-foot Brontosaurus, one of the largest land creatures that ever lived…the giant Tyrannosaurus, the most ferocious flesh-eater of all time.… Stegosaurus 20-feet long with 4 spikes on his tail.…Ankylosaurus, the walking fortress and other prehistoric monsters who ruled the earth some 60 million to 200 million years ago." It seems reasonable that Sinclair had some concerns given that the replicas looked very realistic.

At the completion of this colossal undertaking, on October 15, 1964, Louis Paul Jonas Studios in Churchtown, New York, floated the dinosaurs down the Hudson River to the fair site. The nine dinosaurs were sent floating on an enormously long 320-foot barge in the middle of one of New York's busiest waterways for the near one-hundred-mile voyage. The floating barge caused a massive traffic jam stretching for miles as people stopped to watch this strange sight. After they arrived at the fair's marina, the dinosaurs were trucked to the Sinclair Pavilion site at Flushing Meadows.

Sinclair was hell-bent on making sure its dinosaurs made a splash. After all, the beasts commissioned for the fair were under construction for two years, and the technical team assembled rivaled that of most modern scientific undertakings of the era. Thousands of people lined the streets to view the drama floating down the river. The mighty *Brontosaurus* served as Sinclair's trademark, the symbol of "age and quality" of the crude oils that Sinclair produced and the oil that had been in the earth since the dinosaurs lived. The dinosaur demonstration surely helped sell its products.

At the fair, the Sinclair exhibition of dinosaurs was strategically situated in a vast, prehistoric setting with lifelike flora and fauna. Some of the dinosaurs rested partially in water, as they did in their originally swampy habitat. The nine dinosaurs took two months and $250,000 to complete by opening day, April 22, 1964. Fifty million New York City visitors attended the 1964–65 New York World's Fair, with the Sinclair Corporation's "Dinoland" exhibition among the most popular of all. Fair visitors may recall that Sinclair's "Dinoland" included "Mold-A-Rama" machines that made souvenir dinosaurs for twenty-five cents—"see it formed right before your very eyes." Children watched with fascination as two sides of the mold came together before producing a still warm dinosaur.

Jonas's dinosaurs of Churchtown at the World's Fair. *Wikimedia Commons.*

Several years later, after its World's Fair fame, the Louis Paul Jonas Studio dinosaurs had another life-size *Brontosaurus* make its debut at the thirty-seventh annual Macy's Thanksgiving Day parade on November 23. This dinosaur, unlike the Columbia County version, was in the form of a balloon—in fact, the largest balloon ever displayed in the parade. Sinclair once again commissioned the Jonas Studio for the task. A *Brontosaurus* and baby *Tyrannosaurus rex*, *Stegosaurus* and *Ankylosaurus* all made an appearance in the parade.

Churchtown dinosaurs didn't go extinct. On the contrary, the dinosaurs of Churchtown played a second act in 1965 when it was reported that the Sinclair Company was taking the beasts on an eighteen-state nationwide tour that would last nine months. After the World's Fair and an attempted robbery of two of the coveted dinosaurs, the Jonas team in Churchtown needed to make some repairs. The once-flexible neck of the *Tyrannosaurus rex* needed tending, and sadly it had to be stabilized in a way that the neck no longer moved. Repairing the beast was no easy task. The reproduction dinosaurs were so large that at one time, twenty-eight schoolchildren were able to stand inside them. The amount of intricate detail given to each piece was extraordinary. Sadly, two of the dinosaurs were stolen at the close of the exhibition.

But probably the best part of this famous local story took place on October 5, 1963, just before the fair, when the City of Hudson honored Paul Louis Jonas with a "Dino Day" parade down Warren Street. For his efforts in building such amazing sculptures, Jonas was given the official key to the city.

The parade attracted national attention, with thirty thousand people crowding the streets of Hudson to get a glimpse at the huge creatures, which included the *Struthiosaurus* and others. The parade also featured the American Legion Drum Corps and the Columbian Horseman riding eleven beautiful geldings. People's jaws dropped when the prehistoric monsters sauntered by store windows. Thousands of balloons printed with monsters and the words "Dino Day" sailed through the air. The Continental Cadets band played their instruments, followed by the Royal Blue Angels of Pittsfield, Massachusetts, with the Greenport Rescue squad pulling up the rear. In all, the parade encompassed five divisions. The fire companies escorted the dinosaurs to the Seventh Street Park, where they stayed on display before they were loaded on the barge to head to New York for the World's Fair.

LOST YOUTH: THE VAN WORMER BROTHERS EXECUTED AT DANNEMORA

Willis, Burton and Frederick Van Wormer, along with Harvey Bruce, were accused of brutally killing the Van Wormer boy's uncle, fifty-five-year-old Peter A. Hallenbeck of Greenport near Hudson, New York, on Christmas Eve in the year 1901. Hallenbeck was shot down in cold blood in the doorway of his own kitchen. Remarkably, the heinous crime took place just eighteen miles from Kinderhook, where the boys lived.

Pearl Louise Van Buren was Willis Van Wormer's girlfriend, and the boys' stepmother, Mrs. Van Wormer, along with George H. Brown, a local livery man, and Mrs. Maria Conner, with her two daughters, testified on behalf of the Van Wormer boys, swearing under oath that at the time of the murder, the boys were indeed in Kinderhook and nowhere near the scene of the supposed crime.

On the other side, the prosecution presented Desmond Vernon, a "notion dealer" in Kinderhook, who also swore that on the Monday before the crime was committed, two of the boys now in custody purchased "devil" masks in his store. He even reported that the next day that the boys came back to buy two more. "Devil masks" were part of the local Christmas holiday tradition at the time.

Despite the sworn testimony on their behalf, evidence surfaced that would work against the boys' case. The wheels of a wagon that the youths hired on the day of the murder was said to match the tracks leading from the scene of the crime. It seems that one of the horses driving on the wagon had a peculiar shoe, and the hoofprint found pressed in the snow near the

Hallenbeck home matched perfectly. Because of the matching hoofprint, prosecutors believed that they had the right men, and arrests were made.

Harvey Bruce, the only one of the accused not part of the immediate Van Wormer family, as he was a cousin, made a full confession. According to the *New York Tribune*, Bruce took the stand on April 12 to testify against the other boys.

The testimony of Mrs. Margaret L. Hallenbeck, the wife of the murdered man, explained during court proceedings that four men were involved in the killing, which contradicted earlier reports that only three men shot her husband and one man stayed outside holding the horse near the farm's barn.

On Christmas Eve, Mrs. Hallenbeck was home with her mother-in-law and husband. Early in the evening, she reported, her husband heard the sounds of a wagon approaching the house. Looking out a window, Peter Hellenbeck saw two men walk by his front door wearing black coats. The mysterious visitors then headed toward the nearby church. Just a few minutes later, Mrs. Hallenebeck said that her husband deduced they might have chicken thieves on the property. Soon after, there was a knock on the kitchen door. Mrs. Hallenbeck followed her husband as he went to answer the door.

At that moment, she said that four guns were thrust in Peter Hallenbeck's face, and the assailants, without hesitation, opened fire. Before falling to the shots, Peter pushed his wife out of harm's way. The four men then finished him off with several more shots at close range before Peter could reach his gun to defend himself. Mrs. Hallenbeck said that the men had been wearing their coats turned inside out and that there was a tall one, two medium-sized men and a short one. She made a plea for her husband's life, but seeing that she couldn't save him, she fled for her life, dragging along her eighty-year-old mother-in-law to the attic rooms.

After retrieving the body of Peter Hallenbeck and examining the scene, Sheriff Harry J. Best went to Kinderhook and arrested the three Van Wormer brothers and Harvey Bruce on Christmas Day. Upon conducting a search of the house, they discovered three .32-caliber revolvers and another .36-caliber revolver. To seal the deal, the sheriff took the boys' shoes and matched them perfectly to the tracks left in the Hallenbecks' kitchen. A witness, William Kipp, was at the Dutch Reformed Church on the night of the murder and left when he heard that Hallenbeck had been killed. Later, when he went to his sleigh, he was missing his whip, which later was identified as one of the whips found at the Van Wormer house in Kinderhook.

Another witness, George Greenwood, testified that on Christmas Eve, he saw Harvey Bruce, whom he knew well, get out of a wagon at the Brookside

Hotel in Stockport. Although he called to him, Bruce just turned away, got in his wagon and drove off in the direction of Hudson. Greenwood said that the top was over the wagon and the side curtains were down, so he could not tell if others were inside the wagon.

At the trial in Hudson, the boys said, "They went to their uncle's house for fun…never intending to injure his person," said their lawyer, Mr. Farrar. The attorney contended that the finding of the bullets in the walls and ceilings showed that the boys had no intention of harming Hallenbeck, but that there was a struggle and Hallenbeck produced a weapon. The defense conveyed that in the confusion, a tragedy occurred, one that no one had anticipated. It was reported that "some young women of Hudson, are daily sending flowers to Harvey Bruce. It is probably done to sustain his spirits, which are extremely downcast," said one report.

At court, the boys cried openly. It was reported that even the judge was moved by the "tragic, heart wrenching, soul racking case."

The case was opened in the Columbia County Courthouse on March 31, 1902, and ended on April 18. The press swarmed the area, and the press headquarters was set up in the basement of Evans Hudson Crème Ale Brewery, according to the *Albany Times-Union* on December 25, 1944. From the start, the Van Wormer murder trial at Hudson was noted for the strange defense. Never before had a murderer offer the plea that his crime was merely a practical joke. The jury saw the defense as absurd, yet the Van Wormers did their best to show that they had a valid alibi.

By March 1903, the trial was dragging on in the Supreme Court in Albany nearly two years after the initial crime. New testimony was presented that a family feud existed between the Hallenbecks and the Van Wormers for years. It appeared that while Peter Hallenbeck prospered, his brother-in-law, John Van Wormer, was barely making a living as a Hudson River boatman. Before his untimely death, John Van Wormer managed to buy a small cottage across the road from his brother Peter Hallenbeck's handsome home. The cottage, however, was mortgaged to Hallenbeck.

After John Van Wormer died, Hallenbeck stopped providing financial assistance to his family, and the Van Wormers were forced to move to Kinderhook. This abandonment further fueled the hatred of the Van Wormer brothers for their uncle and was allegedly the motive for the murder.

The trial ended in April, and the boys were given a death sentence for murdering their uncle. The electric chair was the method of execution. Burton Van Wormer, the second in age of the three brothers who were to be executed, made a last-minute plea to save the others by taking full responsibility for the

Mess hall at Clinton Prison, Dannemora, New York. *Library of Congress.*

crime. "I wish it were possible for Gov. Odell to save my brothers' lives," he said to Keeper Joh Healy, one of the "death watchers," "for it was I who killed my uncle. They shot about the room. My bullets were those which killed him."

While awaiting their grim sentence to die, Burt Van Wormer kept his spirits high. In a letter to a friend from his cell, he wrote that he was allowed one hour each day for exercise and "after that he is in solitary confinement." He said he also had the privilege of conversing with his brothers Willis and Fred and that "it goes a great way towards breaking the monotony of prison life." Burton wrote in his letter, "There are few in this wide, wide world who still retain an affectionate regard for us, and I hope and trust that whenever you count your friends my name will be among the favored ones. Kindly remember me to Miss Pearl."

At Dannemora prison, in October 1903, the boys were marched through death row and electrocuted. Their bodies were returned to Kinderhook to the home of Mrs. Estella Van Wormer, their stepmother. As one added gory glitch, even though it seems that Fred Van Wormer's electrocution did take the first time, he was removed from the coroner's room and brought back to the electric chair for two more full charges of current until he was dead for good. Although there was strong opposition on the part of the cemetery commission for selling Mrs. Van Wormer a plot for the interment of her sons, the boys would find their final resting place at the Kinderhook Cemetery, the same place where the body of Martin Van Buren rests.

The three Van Wormer brothers' graves can be found at the Kinderhook Cemetery. They still hold great curiosity for visitors and residents alike. Those who tend to believe in ghosts will tell you that, occasionally, on a cold winter's night near Christmas, four cloudlike beings with "greatcoats" turned inside out, masked and armed with revolvers ride the roads, causing farmers to lend an ear, to be on watch for the Van Wormers who might show up at the kitchen door.

LOST SQUIRE OF GERMANTOWN: GENE SARAZEN

No one naturally puts fruit farming and world-class golfing together, except maybe Gene Sarazen. Gene Sarazen, a golf legend, spent a considerable amount of his life in Columbia County, where he farmed 375 acres of apple orchards and kept Black Angus beef cattle. Ask a few old-timers in the region and they'll tell you stories about his farm, his good nature and his love of Columbia County. They say that Gene worried seasonally about his crops, but he never fretted about his putting. That's because Gene was one of the greatest golfers of all time, and he made his mark on the world in an unusual way.

When he died at age ninety-seven in 1999, Gene Sarazen left a legacy like no other. In the early 1920s and '30s, Sarazen was hailed as one of the finest golfers ever to play the sport. He is perhaps most known for "the shot heard 'round the world"—not related to the opening shot of the Battles of Lexington and Concord in 1775, of course.

"The shot" is directly related to the 1935 Masters Golf Tournament, when Gene Sarazen, using his newly adopted "4-wood," hit a 235-yard golf shot on the fifteenth hole in the fourth round. According to spectators at the famous Augusta, Georgia tournament, the hit flew straight as any shot could and zeroed in on the cup for one of the rarest of all golf shots: a double eagle.

This stunning feat gave Sarazen a score of just two strokes on what was normally a par-five hole! And for anyone who has ever picked up a club and hit the little white ball down the greens, this is as impossible as finding a needle in a haystack.

Sarazen's shot is considered today by most experts to be the single most famous stroke of golf ever to be played. And just for the record, the very next day in that tournament, he defeated Wood in a thirty-six-hole playoff.

Gene Sarazen with his caddy, Stove Pipe. *Bruce Bohnsack, Gibson Photos.*

What's really interesting about this event is that Gene Sarazen reportedly had a conversation with his African American caddy, affectionately called "Stove Pipe" (because he wore a tall Abe Lincoln–style silk top hat), on the day of the great shot. In the 1930s, Black caddies were the norm, especially in places like Augusta, Georgia.

"What do I need to win?" Sarazen asked Stove Pipe as he came to the fifteenth.

"Let's see," said Stove Pipe, "You need four 4, Mr. Sarazen." Par for the hole was 5-34-4. Gene had a good 250-yard drive, but the lie was close. He and Stove Pipe decided that a 4-wood would be used for the 235-yard shot. "I rode into the shot with every ounce of strength I had," Sarazen said. "The split second I hit it, I knew it would carry the pond in front of the green."

But what makes Sarazen's story even more remarkable is his history. Born Egenio Saracini in Harrison, New York, in 1902, Gene was the son of an immigrant Italian carpenter. As was the case with many immigrating to the United States at that time, Gene changed his name because he felt he might fit in better as an American. When the United States entered World War

Gene Sarazen with his family in Germantown. *Bruce Bohnsack, Gibson Photos.*

I in 1917, Gene's father went into debt. It was then that Gene helped his father by doing carpentry work six days a week, and eventually, Sarazen left school during the sixth grade. What happened next changed the trajectory of Gene's life once again.

Tragically, as a teenager, Gene came down with a severe case of pneumonia in 1918 during the influenza pandemic and was unconscious for three days. His recovery was long, and when he was finally released from the hospital, his doctors recommended that he work outdoors. From then on, he started to work as a caddy in Westchester, New York. Going to work on the golf course not only gave Gene an opportunity to be outside in the fresh air but also allowed him to help with the family's financial needs.

Becoming a pro golfer was not necessarily a natural path for Gene. He was small for a golfer, only five feet, five inches, and he had small hands, yet he was gifted. By age twenty, he'd won the first of his two U.S. Open championships in 1922, making him the second-youngest winner in history to take that event. He repeated his victory in the PGA the next year. Sarazen won numerous tournaments in the ensuing years—his total eventually reaching thirty-nine PGA Tour victories.

In 1932, Sarazen began to win even more due to the strength of his new-fangled invention: the sand wedge. Sarazen played a lot of golf, but he also obsessed about the shots he was consistently missing. The losses nagged him so much that he took time out of his game to try to come up with a better way to get his ball out of bunkers. His thought was that he needed a lofted iron, which either used the side of the blade under the ball or a club head that dug into the sand. His moment of genius actually struck while Gene was taking a flying lesson. While looking out the window, he noticed the way in which the plane moved up in the air as the flaps turned down. Sarazen applied the same principle to the sole of a niblick, a lofted iron club. By applying solder to the bottom of the club and filing the sole at a downward angle down at the leading edge, Gene was able to refine the angle so that it traveled smoothly through the sand.

By the winter of 1931, the new-styled club that Sarazen had invented was being used as the modern sand wedge. He introduced his new wedge at the British Open in 1932, and Sarazen's brainchild wedge would go on to change the game of golf forever.

Gene played on as he aged, collecting more and more victories. Sarazen won the PGA Seniors Championship in 1954 and 1958, and in 1963, at age sixty-one, he was the oldest player ever to make the cut in the Augusta Masters. Remarkably, in 1967, Sarazen was still changing the world of golf. He wrote an instructional book for senior players called *Better Golf After Fifty*. He also went on to win the New York State PGA Seniors Championship in 1968.

In 1973, on the fiftieth anniversary of his first British Open, Sarazen wowed the crowd when he scored a hole-in-one on the 126-yard eighth hole at Troon Golf Course. At a time when many golfers stop playing professionally, Gene played into his later years. His career had remarkable longevity. He was sixty-one when he made his final cut at the Masters Tournament. Only Sam Snead beat this record—he made it at the age of sixty-two. When Sarazen was seventy-one, he played his last tournament, where he once again wowed the world by scoring a hole-in-one on the eighth hole during the British Open's first round. Gene Sarazen stands as one of only five professional golfers—along with Ben Hogan, Gary Player, Jack Nicklaus and Tiger Woods—to win each of the four majors at least once, now known as the "Career Grand Slam." In 1996, Gene became the first recipient of the PGA Tour's Lifetime Achievement Award.

Gene Sarazen has a special connection to Columbia County. In 1933, he bought a farm in Brookfield Center, Connecticut, and from that time on, like many young farmers, he became known as "the Squire." He sold the farm in Connecticut in 1944, but with a love of farming, he then purchased a beef and fruit farm in Germantown, New York, in 1945, where he and his family stayed until 1969.

Heralded throughout the county as "the Squire of Germantown," he was best known for his trademark golf knickers, which he continued to wear while working on the farm. To the people of Columbia County, Gene Sarazen was much more than just a golfer.

He farmed hundreds of local acres of apple orchards, and to this day, farmworkers and owners in the apple orchard business remember Gene and his famous golf history. Gene made his home in Columbia County and also became a member of the Columbia County Country Club, where he played often.

LOST VOICES: WHY ELLA SANG THE BLUES

Columbia County has a sordid history. This book and these chapters are a balance of the good with the bad. There's a lot of history we can be proud of, and then there are the stories that some would like to bury, like ghosts, murders, racism and injustice.

One of the stories less spoken of in Columbia County history is that of Ella Fitzgerald, the "Lady Who Sang the Blues." She had her reasons, of course, for singing the blues, and one could have been the time she spent in a Hudson girls' training school. It's a chapter of her life she rarely spoke of, dark days of pain and persecution.

Ella always loved performing. Early on from her childhood days in the early 1900s, when she lived in Newport News, Virginia, Ella wanted to be a dancer, and she adored music. But tragedy struck her early in life. Her mother died in 1932, causing Ella to drop out of school. To survive the neglectfulness she received in her home, Ella made the fateful choice to work in a local brothel, as well as running numbers for her aunt.

In order to escape her abusive stepfather, Ella soon found herself on the street and homeless. It was this twist of fate that caused a judge to sentence Ella to serve three to five years for delinquency at the New York State Training School in Hudson, New York.

In short, the "training" school for girls was a harsh reformatory. The reformatory was established in 1904 as the only institution in New York State that could provide training for delinquent girls under the age of sixteen. These young women were considered inmates like prisoners and were labeled "incorrigible." The label was as harsh as the environment, and sadly, most of the girls had committed no crime at all.

Girls as young as twelve years old were held against their will in this horrid institution. Many of them were simply orphans, abandoned or abused in their homes and sent away. The girls could be committed to the training school by the courts, but also by their families for simply being "ungovernable."

When it was first founded, the New York Training School for Girls was the only institution in New York State to provide training for delinquent girls between twelve and fifteen years old. The institution took over the red-brick buildings and grounds of Hudson's former House of Refuge for Women (1887–1904), which, despite its name, was actually meant to incarcerate women. The prisoners served indeterminate sentences, often as long as five years, for petty larceny, drunkenness and prostitution. The institution was daunting, sitting high on a Hudson River bluff facing west with a million-dollar view of the Catskill Mountains.

Under the New York State Wayward Minor Act, children like Ella could be incarcerated for infractions like skipping school. Girls like Ella were practically jailed for running away from home. As late as the twentieth century, girls could be arrested for "lewd behavior" and "keeping bad company." Progressive reformers in the 1920s and '30s targeted women in their crusades.

At its height, the training school was home to more than four hundred girls. In 1915, John H. Delaney, commissioner of the New York Department of Efficiency and Economy, described the mission of the school: "To accomplish the reformation of wayward girls, to give destitute girls or girls having had improper guardianship right ideas concerning life and its duties…by persuasion and not by punishment."

Fannie French Morse was the superintendent when Fitzgerald arrived at the training school in 1933. Morse rented a farm nearby the school, believing that manual labor would assist in the girls' rehabilitation: "The incorrigible, the emotional, the neurotic, the girl confused with the very tangle of circumstance—in the stabilizing and restoring influences of the farm life many a one can find balance and relief. To the restless girl, calling for another interest, another experience, another adventure before the last is scarce, complete, the numberless and shifting interests and movements of the farm life furnish an almost exhaustless source."

In the early 1930s, around the time Ella was incarcerated there, Morse introduced Hudson's girls to gardening, farming and other outdoor activities. She also engaged Dr. J.L. Moreno to conduct "sociometrics," which involved measuring relationships between white and Black girls.

It was widely reported that Ella hated the reform school from the minute she arrived. She along with other "colored girls" received harsher treatment. First, they were segregated, and later Ella was subject to physical abuse and solitary confinement, a practice that was verified in the institution's annual reports, as well as in New York State investigations.

Clearly, Ella was one of the most famous inmates of the training school. A cast-aside orphan with nowhere to go and no one to care for her, Ella was just sixteen when she arrived at the school, and she stayed for nearly a year. Guilty of nothing more than being homeless, Ella was housed with more than four hundred, about a quarter of whom were young Black women. They were segregated from the rest of the girls and regularly beaten. Thomas Tunney, the last superintendent of the school, wrote that Ella "had been held in the basement of one of the cottages once and all but tortured." Despite the unjust treatment, less than a year after she left the school, Ella would go on to win a talent contest at the legendary Apollo Theater in Harlem. She refused to speak of her experiences at the school for the rest of her life.

Had it not been for an accidental find—remarkably, a box of documents and photographs from the 1920s and '30s about the New York State Training School's young charges unearthed at a yard sale—perhaps none of Ella's harrowing story of this lost year of youth would ever have been told. Ella successfully escaped the training school at the end of 1933.

This excerpt from Nina Bernstein's book *The Lost Children of Wilder: The Epic Struggle to Change Foster Care* references the training school—a "secret cemetery" on the grounds of the school, harsh punishment for escapees and a plantation-like atmosphere for its largely African American inmates in the school's final years:

> *Shirley remembered the stories she had heard from a housemother and some of the girls. They said a secret graveyard lay hidden in the woods on the Hudson grounds. Years ago, dead babies born to inmates were buried there, and bad girls, too—girls caught trying to escape who later died inside the institution. Other bodies were sent home to their folks for burial, but even after death, runaways were punished. This was their solitary confinement: a cold, dark grave lost in the woods forever.*

Part IV

LOST AND FOUND

LOST HORSES: THE SOCIETY FOR
THE PREVENTION OF HORSE THIEVES

To write a book about Columbia County, New York, and not include a chapter about horses would be like forgetting to slather mustard on your hot dog on July 4. The two go hand in hand. From racehorse breeding to fairgrounds trotters, hunt club trials and three-day events, the opportunity to own, breed and compete horses in Old Chatham, Chatham and beyond, historically, is huge.

To put a finer point on the subject, start by looking closely at the old country stores, taverns, stores and blacksmith shops that still exist and you'll see a few old hitching posts in the vicinity. Ask the local merchant if he's ever sold a pair of breeches. In Chatham, the town even boasts its own equestrian movie starlet, Mrs. Floyd Buckley, who appeared in films under the stage name Lillian Ward, celebrated for her famous bareback riding, which she perfected at the Chatham Fair.

Let's begin by getting a few terms right. People in Columbia County don't "horseback ride," they simply "ride." And if want to look like a real "rider," you'd better get some authentic manure on your paddock boots because anyone wearing those spit-shined, imitation Ralph Lauren fashion boots purchased in a Manhattan boutique and not a tack shop simply screams "weekender."

Old Chatham's Pony Club, 1960s. *Library of Congress.*

The towns that generally follow along the Kinderhook Creek—including Chatham, Old Chatham, North Chatham, Chatham Center and East Chatham—have traditionally been referred to as "hunt country." This phrase comes right from old English sport of fox hunting.

For young riders in the 1950s, Old Chatham formed a Pony Club, an offshoot of the British Pony Club, intended to teach young people horsemanship. Dues in those days were just $2.50 per year. Today, the Old Chatham Hunt Club members still ride the pastoral landscapes, traipsing after foxes and drawing out coyotes, rabbits and the occasional bear.

But all that pomp and circumstance aside, if you want to go back in time and discover the real riders of the region, we need to talk about the Society for the Detection of Horse Thieves. The society was established for the purpose of recovering stolen horses and apprehending the thieves—to "carry the same into effect, a number of riders are engaged to go immediately in pursuit of stolen horses at the expense of the Society."

Now, these guys weren't fancy, but they could ride like hell. Their method for apprehending thieves was to form a rudimentary posse. They used telegraph messages and the telegram to keep their location known, get up-to-the-minute instructions and give details to other riders on the hunt for thieves. The methods were slow and costly, and there were plenty of times where money was exhausted and so were the riders.

The society was originally organized in 1799 and for many years was active in the apprehension of horse thieves on a weekly and often daily basis. If apprehended, the thieves were sometimes hanged. With this threat of death, the society members sought to warn off potential rustlers, believing that thieves might keep clear, and especially safeguard any horse belonging to a society member.

The local papers frequently reported incidents where horses were stolen. In 1894, the Hudson, New York *Columbia Republican* noted:

> *HAS A STOLEN HORSE. A Telegraph lineman Captured with the Property in the City. John W. Hoes, of Columbiaville, reported to Chief of Police Snyder morning, of the 10th, that two telegraph linemen who were temporarily boarding at his hotel broke into the barn soon after midnight and stole a bay horse and a backboard wagon. He traced the property to this city and saw the horse and a strange wagon on Warren street. Policeman Shepard and special officer McManamy made a search for the horse thieves and one of them was captured at a saloon, where a stop had been made for drinks. A downtown young man who has figured conspicuously in several scrapes was in company with the fellow having the horse. When arraigned in Police Court the one arrested said his name was B. William Donnelly. He denied that he took the horse and wagon from Mr. Hoes, but intimated*

Rounding up horse thieves. *Library of Congress.*

that a friend named Kelly, who came with him to Hudson, might know something about the taking of the property. A friend of the latter soon appeared and a proposition was made to Mr. Hoes that if a settlement could be affected Kelley might possibly be found. While an effort was being made to find Kelley his companion was sent to jail and will have a further examination to-day. The exchange of wagons was made in this city. Mr. Boss's buckboard wagon, with a wheel gone, was found near the river, where an exchange had been made in the night for a vehicle owned by a peddler of notions. The peddler said it was the first time anyone ever made a trade with him that he got stuck.

While horse thieving persisted, some of the horse thief societies had fallen off by 1914, but the Schodack, Stuyvesant, Kinderhook and Chatham Societies established in 1824 persevered. By the 1940s, the riders were performing different duties.

Fast-forward to today and you'll find that the groups still meet annually to test their equestrian abilities by pursuing "possible thieves" on horseback. The members still work from the original rules. The position of "riders" must be selected from the society's constitution. According to the official documents, the rider must be called on to go out in pursuit of a thief or thieves, provide his own mount and while on the road of such duties shall not be paid in excess of two dollars per day for their expenses.

LOST IN THE WOODS: ANIMALS IN OUR PAST

A number of wild creatures, both large and small, have lived in Columbia County throughout our history. One of the more notable animals roaming our land is the beaver. Beaver, and their furs, were one of the main reasons that the Dutch originally settled along the Hudson River. In fact, it was Henry Hudson's report of the great abundance of furs found in the river valley (later named for him) that started the Dutch settlement.

In 1610, a ship was deployed from Amsterdam to collect beaver pelts along what the Dutch called the "Groote Rivier," or the Great River, and by 1611, tremendous fur trading had started at the very place that Henry Hudson's ship, the *Half-Moon*, had anchored near Albany. The New Netherlands Company was created in 1614 for the express purpose to corner the market on beaver trading. It claimed all trading rights in the

Sketch of beavers of Columbia County. *Library of Congress.*

lands east of the river where Henry Hudson had explored. The Dutch West India Company, which first employed Henry Hudson to make his famous voyage of discovery, was granted a twenty-four-year monopoly to develop the entire Western Hemisphere from Brazil to New Netherlands. One could argue that the simple beaver started the settlement of the entire New World.

Locally, one of the early settlers, Abraham Statts, was a "Beaverwyck" (what we now call Albany) fur trader. Upward of forty-five thousand beaver pelts were shipped yearly from Beaverwyck to New York City in the early 1600s. Due to the extraordinarily high volume of pelts sought and sold, beavers became nearly extinct in our county by the 1700s. Now and then, you'll see a beaver in the county at the edge of the Kinderhook Creek, in a local marshy stream or bog. In addition to the beaver, New York City was hungry for game to adorn their dinner plates. City folk in that period ate deer, squirrels and wild turkeys. Ads would boast the best game as coming from "upstate." The desire for deer and other creatures made hunting season a huge recreational activity. The hunting for deer was so rigorous that neighbors feared for their lives, and deer were very hard to find by the 1900s.

Native animals come and go in Columbia County. Butterflies like the mighty Monarchs, Red Admirals and Painted Ladies make a north–south migration. The same is true for dragonflies, fish and a number of bird species.

THE LOST ONE-ROOM SCHOOLHOUSE

In the early days of Columbia County, children gathered in one-room schoolhouses for their lessons. All of the students met together, with just one teacher for the whole group. Columbia County once had more than one hundred school districts, each of which erected its own little schoolhouse, with the last one closing back in 1965. If you take a drive around, you can still see the schoolhouses and traces of some that have been rebuilt and reconstructed for houses. Some have burned, and some have been taken simply by time. Some are still standing, including the Ichabod Crane Schoolhouse in Kinderhook.

This one is unique. It isn't the oldest, but it has the most unusual story. It was constructed around 1850, and it's still visible from Route 9-H. It's simple and white and now operates as part of Columbia County's museums. Before it took its current white clapboard schoolhouse form, it was a log cabin school where the famous Jesse Merwin taught school. Merwin was a friend of Washington Irving's and proved to be the inspiration for the one and only Ichabod Crane character in Irving's famous story "The Legend of Sleepy Hollow." The schoolhouse didn't start on this spot. It was moved to its current location after it closed for good in the 1940s. Nevertheless, and despite its reworking, it's still a great example of the area's one-room schoolhouse. Inside you'll find one big room, which served as the single classroom. It has a big wood stove, wooden floors and a chalkboard that, as you would imagine, drew the children's attention daily. Not surprisingly, folks in the region still remember attending "Ichabod Crane schoolhouse" in Kinderhook. What's even more interesting is that Eleanor Roosevelt made a quick visit back in the 1950s. As everyone knows, Eleanor loved to drive her car, and she loved to report on her travels during her radio broadcasts. The school became a topic of one of Eleanor's radio shows.

Although the schoolhouse was white, most are red. There's a reason why schoolhouses were usually painted red. The red schoolhouse dates back to the Civil War era, after log buildings were phased out. One story tells us that when iron ore was ground down, it could be used as a color pigment, and this became an inexpensive way to use red in paint for barns. The iron pigment was mixed with buttermilk. The casein works the same way in today's paints. In essence, the paint was inexpensive to make and use, so schools as well as barns were painted red.

LIVINGSTON AND THE LOST GOLD
OF CAPTAIN KIDD

For nearly four centuries, treasure hunters have searched for any possible remains of Captain Kidd's infamous pirated loot. Rumors abound that Columbia County's own Robert Livingston, Lord of the Manor, was intricately involved in this infamous episode.

Captain William Kidd was commissioned by William III of England in 1695 as a "privateer." His primary job was to hunt and capture pirates on the open seas. It was Robert Livingston who mastermind this unusual agreement because, of course, there was something in it for him. The arrangement was that Kidd and Livingston were to receive a 10 percent share of the profits recovered from any treasure Kidd obtained pirates. One tenth would be turned over to the king, and most of the rest was to be given to an administrator and various investors; anything that remained was divided among Kidd's crewmen.

Robert Livingston was a young Scotsman who popped up in Albany in the late 1600s with one thing in mind: getting rich. And Robert Livingston did just that. He became the first clerk of the city. Although he was the founder of the aristocratic Livingston clan, few knew that he partnered with Captain William Kidd. And even fewer people knew that it was Livingston who hatched the plan to form a company and send out a ship to stop the pirates, employing Kidd as its skipper.

In the latter part of the seventeenth century, the Hudson River was home to a band of ruthless pirates who lured cargo ships into the many coves and harbors that dot the shorelines of the north part of the river. These coves were right in Robert Livingston's backyard, in the area of Columbia County.

Because it infuriated Livingston that pirates would have the audacity to raid ships so close to his mansion and possibly jeopardize his property and family, he took steps to stop the pirates. He personally contributed to a fund that had as its purpose the eradication of the brazen men who flew the "Jolly Roger" from their masts.

In the year 1696, Robert L. Livingston, ancestor of the Livingstons of New York, found himself in England on business connected to the colonies in America. On that trip, he bumped into Lord Bellomont, who had just been appointed the governor of Massachusetts Bay and New Hampshire. The chance encounter put the two men into an unusual conversation. The subject of their talk was solving the problem of how American provinces could protect themselves from the acts of pirates, which at that time were common to the waters of Massachusetts Bay and Long Island Sound as well as the coast of the Atlantic.

Livingston suggested that there be a policy of sending an armed vessel, with a worthy commander, in search of these looters and thieves. In short, they wanted to hire an equally cunning and ruthless thief to hunt down the criminals. Livingston then went on to introduce the name of a fellow countryman, a Scot like himself, Captain William Kidd, as just the right man to lead this needed work. He went on to describe Kidd as a "man of integrity and courage, well acquainted with the pirates." He said he was certain that Kidd would take on the assignment if the king would give him a good sailing vessel equipped with thirty guns and 150 men.

Captain William Kidd in chains.
Library of Congress.

The proposition was sent to William III, king of England in 1695, who sent it to the governor-elect. It was decided by Bellomont and Livingston to embark on a joint venture moneymaking scheme. They called it a joint stock "speculation," meaning the men would take a "share" in the rich returns in the spoils of the buccaneers. Robert Livingston engineered the arrangement in which Kidd and Livingston were to receive 10 percent share of the profits recovered for any treasure obtained from pirates.

Before departing, Captain Kidd had a document in his possession that empowered him to "'act against the King's enemies,' and take prizes from them as a private man of war; to procure from the King a grant to be made of some 'Indifferent and trusty person' of all such merchandise, goods and treasures, as shall be taken from the said 'pirates' by Kidd, or any other ship under his command; to pay 4/5 of all money's which shall be laid out in the purchasing and equipping such a ship the other fifth to be paid by Livingston and Kidd in order the speedy buying of such a ship." Kidd agreed to eventually make his way to Boston in New England and there deliver up whatever goods he seized to the Earl of Bellomont. Kidd and Livingston also would have a piece of the spoils.

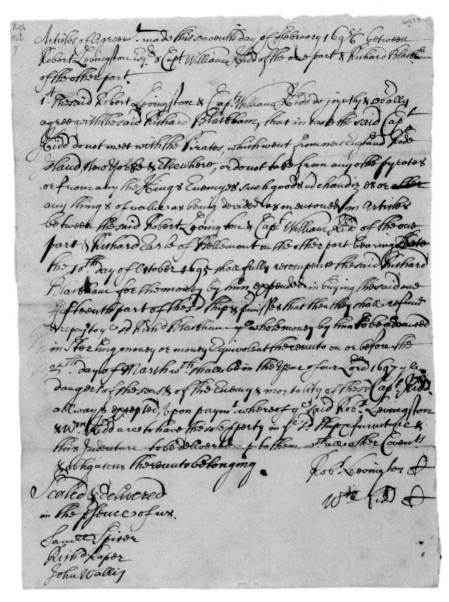

Above: Kidd's letter of agreement with Livingston. *Library of Congress.*

Following: Captain Kidd in New York Harbor. *Library of Congress.*

Robert Kidd took over command of the *Adventure Galley* and sailed on in April 1696 from Plymouth to New York, carrying thirty guns and eighty men. It was the wish of King William that Kidd not only destroy the "freebooters" but also take any French merchantmen he might find as well. King William, at the time, was at war with France. True to his promise, Kidd captured a French "banker" ship, which he carried into New York and sold.

Kidd's promise to his crew was that each man on the ship was to share a certain rate in the proceeds of the cruise. Kidd then headed to Madagascar in February, a place thick with pirates. While his first intent was to cruise the coast of America, his employers sent him there because of possible higher gains; instead, it proved a waste of time. In the meantime, discouraged by their lack of success, Kidd's men were becoming restless. Kidd's employers, Livingston and Bellomont, were growing unhappy too and considered dismissing him from his command. Nervous that his crew was not benefiting from raiding ships, Kidd feared that a mutiny was brewing so he promised his men that a better fortune could be had if they remained obedient to his orders. They agreed, believing that a rich prize was coming soon. Kidd sailed his ship to the Malar Islands, where they soon encountered a Moorish fleet. Kidd attacked, but the fleet pursued and Kidd turned back. Still determined not to be driven off until he had robbed at least one of the smaller ships, Kidd overtook a vessel and forced two of the crew on the ship to join his men. The remaining men on the ship Kidd whipped unmercifully, forcing them to confess the whereabouts of their money. Kidd then took everything of value, and the ship was permitted to return to the fleet.

The report of the piracy spread like wildfire along the coast, and Portuguese ships were dispatched to apprehend this new sea robber. Kidd's vessel, the *Adventure Galley*, engaged with the ships, and both lost many men. For a while, Kidd held on, confident that he would prevail, but the Portuguese were too strong. Eventually, he turned his boat around and was able to outrun his enemies.

Knowing that his activities as a pirate would eventually lead him to the gallows, Kidd searched for a way that he could abandon his criminal life. But just about then, he ran across a Dutch ship carrying valuable cargo. Knowing that he was fully unprepared to fight the ship, Kidd let the vessel pass untouched. Kidd's men accused him of taking a bribe from the Dutch skipper as a condition of his granting them safety. Kidd's crew threatened to mutiny and take command of the ship, but Kidd put a quick end to the dispute by pulling his pistol and shooting the ringleader dead. With that, Kidd rapidly plundered a long line of vessels at sea, satisfying his crew and earning the reputation of a pirate and one of the most feared commanders on the open sea.

It wasn't long before Kidd was reaping the benefits of his adventures. What he wasn't counting on was that Bellomont, in Boston, was protesting loudly about pirate activity in New York. At the time, Kidd was carrying an enormous treasure, and he attempted to make a deal with Bellomont to declare that he was innocent of crimes of piracy. In return, Kidd promised him a share of the mounting gold and jewels in his treasure. With this plan in mind, Kidd sent a crewman named Emot to Boston to see if Bellomont would agree and waited for a reply on Block Island, just off the coast of Connecticut in the Long Island Sound.

It's said that while Kidd sat waiting on Block Island, three mysterious sloops visited him. For some time, it was rumored that they left with a portion of Kidd's treasure. Finally, Emot returned with a message from Bellomont. He would agree to promise Kidd protection only if he could prove that he had the treasure he claimed.

What happened next would have treasure hunters around the world looking for gold. Before he set off to see Bellomont in Boston, Kidd decided to hide his portion of the treasure. He sought out his friend John Gardiner, who was living on a nearby manor on Gardiners Island (a part of the New York Long Island Hamptons). There, Kidd deposited his precious gold and silver.

When word spread that Kidd was suspected of piracy, Livingston feared that their plan would be revealed and he too would be implicated as a pirate and criminal. Parliament, for its part, did everything in its power to keep word from spreading that the king and admiralty took any part in a gun-for-hire operation.

As Kidd headed to Boston from the Caribbean, Livingston informed the lieutenant governor of New York that Kidd was carrying treasure. Kidd was captured and sent to England for trial in May 1701. When he reached Boston, he was arrested for piracy and sent back to England to be hanged at the gallows.

HOW OLD CHATHAM LOST ITS NAME
AND FOUND A NEW ONE

About 240 years ago, the easternmost part of Chatham was called New Britain; a deed of 1784 gives as a boundary line "the road running easterly to New Britain." This probably included the hamlet we know as Old Chatham, once called "The Corners" and during the War of 1812 "Federal Stores," later called Chatham.

Old Chatham sits at the crossroads of the old Albany Turnpike and County Route 13 and is perhaps the oldest settlement in the town of Chatham. For some time, it was the most important community in the area. There were several sawmills in the town and four inns that supplied lodging for travelers on the Albany Pike, which passed through the village. The earlier name of the hamlet, Federal Stores, was derived from the fact that there existed here one of the nation's first cooperative stores, which we know today as the Old Chatham Country Store.

The Federal Stores establishment opened in 1767, and the store was organized on the cooperative plan by a group of Columbia County men, one of whom was James Roosevelt, the late President Theodore Roosevelt's great-grandson. A rumor circulated that the name Federal Stores was applied because during the Civil War, the government had a small ammunition depot there that stored gunpowder and bullets for use of the troops in the Union army.

The Federal Stores establishment in the early days was a fairly large place, with lots of products to buy as well as fresh produce that was shipped in from hundreds of miles away by refrigerated railroad cars. Stephen Wilbor had a store in a building that remained the property of members of that family for a great many years. In 1810, Thomas Hoag kept a store in a part of the building in which he also had a tavern. Other later merchants who occupied Federal Stores included A. Campbell, David Carshor, Harvey Brown, Benjamin Rider, Seth Daley, C.B. Hudson and others. The Wait brothers opened a hardware store that lasted forty years, and J.W. Redmond was one of the more recent merchants. A pioneer gristmill was built at Federal Stores and burned in 1875.

Patrons of the store could buy everything from raisins and currants to flour, superfine or common rice, brown sugar, green tea, Bohea and Hyson tea and coffee by a hundred pounds or less. Most of the time, the store had on hand fine extracts and spices like citron, almonds, mace, ground ginger, pepper, allspice, basket salt and cayenne pepper. People also flocked to the

Old Chatham historical marker. *Author's photo.*

store to buy very fine chocolate by the box or the pound, and of course, there was tobacco or snuff for those who preferred it. The store had nothing perishable since it did not have a refrigerator, and the vacuum sealing process that would preserve food in an aluminum can had yet to be invented.

When the store was first created, Old Chatham, then known as Chatham, was still only a very small settlement of houses; consequently, most of the customers traveled from other towns. Because of the difficult transportation (roads through Columbia County were few, and the ones that did exist were unpaved and in extremely poor condition) and the fact that traveling took so long, people were not able to get to the store very often. Therefore, when families did come the long distance to reach the store, they purchased a supply of goods that would last them weeks and even months and returned to their homes with barrels in their horse-drawn carriages.

The Federal Stores was not without its troubles. Papers ran news like this headline in the Sentinel, New York *Kinderhook* in 1842: "The store of Seth Daley, Esq., at Federal Stores, Chatham was forcibly entered one night last week, and about ten dollars in all was stolen out of the money drawer."

With the growth of the population of the villages in surrounding areas, other stores sprang up. Eventually, the Federal Stores cooperative store began to lose customers and prestige and finally ceased to exist at all. However, during the years of its life, it had been an exceedingly lucrative enterprise for its founders, and it was not completely forgotten for a long time because for years afterward people continued to call it Old Chatham or Federal Stores. Due to the success of the cooperative, the hamlet itself became known as Federal Stores, a name it retained until Chatham Township became incorporated in 1795.

If we look into the hamlet's past, we'll find that Old Chatham was established in the early 1750s by people from Lyme, Connecticut, named Tubbs and Hudson, along with the Alger and Huntley families. They were joined by others from Dutchess County who cleared land, and then pioneer families began to establish farms. Of course, as with all pioneers, this resulted in contested claims by the patents of the Westerbrook Grant and John I. Van Rensselaer, who claimed ownership and demanded the settlers become tenants.

In 1774, the farmers of Old Chatham initiated court action to obtain title to their lands and sent James Savage to England to obtain satisfaction for their claims. The Revolutionary War cut short his appeals, and it was not until 1778 that the Canaan Act confirmed the settlers' titles to the lands. During the Revolution, the local militia drilled and paraded in the Old Chatham square, and it was here the Federal Stores Company was established in 1787 on the site of the present post office.

Now, if you look carefully, you'll find a few of the mile markers along the road still visible in the area because postage was collected according to the distance a letter traveled. Many of the older structures in the square in Old Chatham are former inns, stores or public houses. Jackson's Old Chatham House restaurant was formerly Wait Bros. hardware emporium, while the residence adjacent was an inn.

Just behind Jackson's stands a former blacksmith shop, last occupied by Ben Cole, the last of a long line of farriers in the Cole family. The little red blacksmith's building is still visible today.

In the 1780s, the first Samuel Wilbor took up residence in the community. He would influence the hamlet's industrial and religious life for nearly 125 years until the last Samuel Wilbor died in 1905. It was the second Samuel Wilbor who built the impressive brick residence in Old Chatham that stands next to the pond and what was once called Mirror Lake in the early 1800s. An early tavern was opened on the site of the later Locust Tree House by Thomas Hoag; it received large patronage from the many travelers over the turnpike on which it was situated. Several other public houses were opened at different dates, and one hotel is still run today. At one point, the post office here was moved from Malden Bridge, but the date for that is uncertain. Among the physicians who practiced here prior to recent years were Dr. Horace Root, who died in Chatham in 1865, and Dr. N.M. Ransom.

Back in the day, Old Chatham was the site of the Lebanon Springs railroad, which first served Old Chatham. It later became the Rutland Railroad, which ran northward into Vermont. The depot was a busy location, handling the shipping of milk from a station at the end of Depot Lane. The old depot, now a private home, is still visible in Old Chatham.

Farmers brought milk to the train station, operated by the Borden Company. There it was cooled and then sent on to Chatham and to New York City on the Harlem Division Railroad. The railroad had a busy passenger service, as it served as a commuter line for local students and shoppers going to and from Chatham. Sadly, the residents of Old Chatham heard the Rutland's mournful whistle for the very last time in 1959, when rail service was terminated.

In 1869, an interesting fight broke out between the Village of Chatham and Federal Stores. Both the present Chatham village and today's Old Chatham claimed the name Chatham. Chatham Village officers had a meeting and were so determined to claim the name that they took the matter to court in Hudson. A contingent representing Chatham (Old) planned to fight for the name, so they planned to take the Rutland Railroad (which ran through Old Chatham) to Chatham and then transfer to a Hudson Division train to attend court in the county seat of Hudson. That particular day, the Rutland Line was running late, and subsequently, the Old Chathamites missed their connection. When the judge heard the matter in his court, he asked, "Where are the other Chatham people?" Because of their absence, he ruled in favor of the village, which kept the name Chatham. The "other Chatham" became Old Chatham.

When you're in the area, stop by the "new" Old Chatham Country Store. It has a fine group of proprietors who will serve you a hearty lunch at a fair price.

LOST TO HISTORY: CAVALRY LIEUTENANT JOHN BLUNT, CHATHAM'S CIVIL WAR HERO, AND PETER WHEELER, SLAVE OF SPENCERTOWN

Up a rather steep hill, out of sight from the Main Street in Chatham, there is an expansive rural cemetery. The cemetery is old, surrounded by ancient hemlocks, and there's a tranquil pond in the distance.

Many years ago, the president of the United States, in the name of Congress, awarded the Medal of Honor to First Lieutenant John W. Blunt, U.S. Army, for extraordinary heroism. He received the award on October 19, 1864, while serving with Company K, Sixth New York Cavalry, due to action at Cedar Creek, Virginia. First Lieutenant Blunt voluntarily led a charge on horseback across a narrow bridge over the Cedar Creek, fearlessly facing the enemy head on.

It was cold on October 19, 1864, when Brigadier General Thomas C. Devin, commanding the Second Brigade, Sixth New York Cavalry, took his officers into his tent and discussed what they were going to do next. They stood on the outskirts of Middletown, Virginia, in the midst of the Civil War. He told his men that he had been ordered along a turnpike that skirt and that he was to connect his forces with lines of the Union infantry that had been fighting their way into Middletown. Both the Sixth and the First New York Cavalry had charged twice into the town but were held back by the Confederates, who had been hiding behind brick garden walls and secure enclosures. Despite the Union army's fierce attempts, they were "compelled to retire under terrible fire," and they found it impossible to reach the enemy forces.

At approximately 2:30 p.m. on the afternoon of the nineteenth, Devin called another conference with his staff, but the group broke up quickly as they began to take on enemy fire on its right side, the side of the turnpike leading into Middletown. They tried again to fight but were forced back once again.

General Devin, seeing no way in using the turnpike, ordered his men to bypass to the left of the town and advance as quickly as possible toward Cedar Creek. It was then 3:00 p.m. when the order came to move down to the creek in an effort to overtake enemy forces on the opposite bank.

John Blunt portrait. *Wikimedia Commons.*

As the troops approached the creek, they could see the bridge ahead. It was so narrow that only two horses could pass riding abreast. The bridge spanned about 150 feet in length and was about 30 feet high. Before Company K could make a decision as how to attack, Confederate riflemen opened fire at point-blank range. At that moment, a young Union cavalry officer, Lieutenant John Blunt of Chatham, Four Corners, New York, "straightened his saddle, and above the roar of the musketry, shouted, Bugler, sound the charge!"

Facing grave danger, the brave men of Company K charged toward the bridge. Instantly, horses and riders fell to the oncoming fire, yet by some miracle, the bearded young officer leading the charge was unscathed as his horse galloped across the Cedar Creek bridge, followed by the bugler and a dozen riders.

Once across the bridge, and with bullets in the air, Lieutenant Blunt and his platoon dodged enemy fire and jumped their horses over a stone wall, engaging in hand-to-hand fighting with the Confederates. The enemy, stunned to see so many horses and riders within inches, ran for the nearby woods. As a result, the Sixth and First Cavalries continued at full gallop toward the forest and encircled the town of Middletown, thus winning the

Battle of Cedar Creek. It was the daring work of the young officer, John W. Blunt, who won the fight and would receive the Congressional Medal of Honor for his bravery that day.

He was born in Stuyvesant Landing, New York, in 1840. His family moved to Austerlitz when he was a young boy. Like most young men of the day, he had little schooling and went to work on his father's farm. In October 1861, when he turned twenty-one years old, John joined his brothers, Rusten, Robert and Joseph and took the train from Chatham to Hudson to enlist in the Union forces.

He was tall and slim, by most descriptions a gallant young man with a long flowing mustache and goatee. He joined Company M, Sixth New York Cavalry, and was quickly recognized as an able leader. He was promoted first to sergeant and then to second lieutenant by March 1863, and he earned his silver bars in December. In recognition of the Cedar Creek charge, he was elevated to the rank of captain on October 21, 1864.

Captain Blunt was then transferred to the Second Provisional Cavalry in June 1865 and was made a major of New York Volunteers. He was mustered out with his company on August 9, 1865, at Louisville, Kentucky.

When Blunt returned to Chatham, he became a beloved and legendary figure, riding his horse at the Chatham Fair. At the annual fair, he served as grand marshal at the parades and always wore his campaign hat cocked over one eye in traditional cavalry style. Captain Blunt retained his good looks and was quite dashing in his blue uniform and red sash. Parade attendees were most impressed when they saw his glistening saber, which he carried throughout the Civil War, hanging from his saddle. The Medal of Honor recipient was always happy to be a part of Memorial Day remembrances and celebrations, and he organized the General John A. Logan Post GAR, which met at the Masonic Hall on Park Row.

Tragedy struck in 1910 when, at age seventy, Captain Blunt took a terrible fall in his Chatham home. As was his daily routine, he got up before dawn. Sadly, on his way to the kitchen, he plunged head first down the stairs in his home. The fall caused a severe head injury, and a surgeon was immediately called to perform an operation to relieve pressure on his brain.

Sadly, the Civil War hero of Chatham never regained consciousness and succumbed to the injury. He was laid to rest by surviving members of the GAR at the Chatham Rural Cemetery.

PETER WHEELER, LIKE CAPTAIN John Blunt, holds a unique place in Columbia County's history. He was not a Civil War hero like John Blunt; rather, he was enslaved, born in 1789, and escaped bondage.

In 1806, he settled in Spencertown, New York. He would go on to publish an autobiography that described in detail his experience of being enslaved, *Chains and Freedom: or The Life and Adventures of Peter Wheeler, A Colored Man Yet Living. A Slave in Chains, A Sailor on the Deep, And a Sinner at the Cross. Three Volumes in One by the Author of The Mountain Wild Flower.*

Peter Wheeler portrait. *Library of Congress.*

Published in 1839, it was written by an abolitionist named Charles Edwards Lester of Spencertown, pastor of St. Peter's Church. Lester befriended Peter and wrote down his story in a series of interviews. In the preface to the book, Charles and Peter state that the goal in sharing Wheeler's experience was to contribute "to the freedom of enchained millions." It was also clearly stated that while it was Lester who technically performed the writing of the book, the narrative was "taken entirely from the lips of Peter Wheeler." Lester also makes the point in the preface that Wheeler's personal remembrances are supported by the "hundreds of living witnesses" who were friendly with Wheeler and heard him tell his stories.

Wheeler explained in his autobiography that to the best of his recollection, he was born on January 1, 1789, in Tuckertown, New Jersey. He recalled the stories his mother told him about how his great-grandfather was born in Africa. One day, while collecting seashells on the beach with his sister, a boat with white sailors approached and captured them. They were brought to a large ship, where many other Africans had been taken. The ship traveled over the ocean toward America. The two young Africans found themselves in Baltimore, where they were sold at auction.

As the story is told, Wheeler's mother was a slave who was freed in her former owner's will, but after Peter was born, he was taken by a white family named Mather, who had just lost a baby who was around the same age. The mother originally wanted Peter so that she could have a baby to nurse; when Peter's mother asked to have her boy back, the mother said no.

Job Mather put Peter to work doing laundry, cooking, carrying dinner out to the field hands and other chores. Peter wrote in his book that he always had enough to eat and that he was close with the family's two sons,

Peter Wheeler historical marker. *Library of Congress.*

playing and getting into mischief. When Peter was eleven years old, Mrs. Mather died. Seeing her buried was terribly painful, he wrote: "When I see her laid in the grave it broke my heart." Once she died, Wheeler said that he "had nothin to expect from master," and he was "left in the world friendless and alone."

Distraught and pained by the loss of his wife, Job Mather put his entire plantation up for sale, and despite the fact that Wheeler was "free by law," he was sold for $110 to a man by the name of Gideon Morehouse. Peter then moved with his new master to western New York.

Morehouse was an abusive man, frequently beating Peter, whipping him and neglecting his needs. At one point, Wheeler became ill with typhus fever because Morehouse left him without food in a place with no heat. He nearly starved and froze to death through the winter. Wheeler said that he was beaten so often over a five-year period that his wounds never healed. With no other choice, Wheeler planned his escape over a four-year period while enduring horrendous conditions and physical abuse. He wrote that he decided to be free or "die in the cause."

One Sunday in 1806, Peter made his escape, traveling down toward Oneida Lake to southern New York, where he met a boat captain and became part of the ship's crew. After years as a crew member traveling the world, Peter headed toward New York City. In the city, he found odd jobs and was able to make money. He eventually met, fell in love with and married Solena Nixon. Not long after their marriage, however, Solena died suddenly. The loss was devastating, and Peter began to wander without direction.

He traveled to Sharon, Connecticut, where he stayed for six months tending a sawmill. There he met another African American man by the name of Joshua Nichols. Nichols was married to a lovely woman. After they had a child, Nichols abandoned them and went to Columbia County, New York. Peter set out one day for Albany, but before he departed, he met a woman who asked him if he could find her husband in New York. The woman turned out to be Joshua Nichols's wife.

Since he was going that way, Peter agreed, so he left Sharon and headed to Spencertown, where he found Nichols. Peter asked him upon meeting why he abandoned his wife in such a cruel way. Instead of answering him, Joshua simply gave him a letter and paid Peter to deliver it to his wife back in Sharon. When Mrs. Nichols read the letter, she instantly burst into tears, learning that her husband had no plan to return to her. Peter never did travel to Albany; instead, he went back to Spencertown, where he met Erastus Pratt, who hired him.

"When I got to Erastus Pratt's he wanted to hire me six months, and I hired, and his family was nice folks, and he had a whole fleet of gals, and they was all as find as silk, but I used to tell Aunt Phebe, that Harriet was the rather the nicest." Peter stayed many years in Spencertown, the place where he would eventually meet Lester and write his story.

A historical marker stands on the end of Dugway Road in Spencertown near where Peter Wheeler lived until 1839.

LOST LANDLORD—FOUND MURDERED: WHAT HAPPENED TO ALONZO COOK?

Throughout its history, Columbia County was a thriving rural haven. Ancram, in the southern portion of Columbia County, was a tiny little hamlet with nothing more than a main street, a paper mill and a few lead mines. One day in 1908, something quite strange occurred at the Central New England Railroad stop. It was one of the early morning station agents who discovered a virtual "Noah's Ark" aboard a series of gold and white boxcars.

Leaving the train cars, standing side by side, were camels and huge white horses followed by a long row of ponies. The animals formed a circus parade, lined up in pairs down the main street. The local citizens were stunned to see the Barnum & Bailey Circus. The Greatest Show on Earth had arrived.

Apparently, the circus had outgrown its winter home of Bridgeport, Connecticut, and had advertised for someone with large barns to care for some of the stock over the winter months. One of the men who answered the ad was Alonzo Cook Jr., a descendant of an old Columbia County family who resided on a 350-acre farm near Ancram.

Alonzo just loved all kinds of animals and had some of the finest dairy cows in the county on his farm. When Alonzo saw the ad, he felt certain that he could easily care for a few more horses and the circus entourage. He agreed to board the horses and stock for a mere twenty dollars per month. He continued to live in his farm house, happy with his animals on the farm, until he was about eighty-six years old.

On the morning of June 17, 1949, a neighbor spotted smoke coming out of a section of the house where he was living, but it wasn't the smoke that killed him. An examiner discovered a wide gash at the base of Alonzo's skull. He died within minutes of receiving the blow.

Several years earlier, Alonzo Cook sold his expansive farm to a fifty-eight-year-old retired navy captain named Steven Williams. At the time, Alonzo was getting old; he was eighty-four, and although the house and farm had been in his family for many generations, he found it hard to handle alone. Alonzo was lonely and broke, so when Williams showed up, it was like a godsend.

Cook learned about Williams, who was visiting Ancram, and after many letters, they arranged the sale. Williams agreed to purchase the farm for $35,000. He gave Cook a fairly small down payment of only $2,500. This transaction took place in early September 1947. The deal required that Williams pay Cook monthly installments of $5,000 until the debt was paid. As another part of the deal, Cook would hold the mortgage and be allowed to live in a cramped apartment that had been built on the far side of the house. Cook could live out his life there on his family farm. A couple, Ward and Edna Oakley, and their four children were also tenants in the house. The wife performed household duties and cooked, while her husband did chores on the farm. To Alonzo Cook, the situation was nothing less than perfect.

No one doubted that Williams was an upstanding man. He wore a meticulously groomed white goatee and boasted an impeccable naval uniform. He explained to the people in the town that he had graduated from the finest U.S. Naval Academy at Annapolis and had fought bravely in several naval battles, including one in the Baltic in World War I, and had seen action during World War II. For all intents and purposes, Williams was a local hero. The market owner and other shopkeepers called him "Captain." Town officials insisted that he lead all of the patriotic ceremonies like the

Fourth of July parade and ceremonies on Memorial Day. He was even a favorite presenter at Boy Scout jubilees.

Sometimes, however, if a situation looks too good to be true, it is. Trouble started in October 1948 when Williams failed to make his scheduled mortgage payment to Cook. Making no elaborate excuses, Williams simply told the old man that he couldn't pay, and Cook seemed satisfied with a promise of money to come soon. Yet within weeks, Williams took out an insurance policy on the farm buildings that covered the place in case of fire.

Not more than one month later, one of the barns of the farm burned to the ground, and Williams used the settlement money to pay his mortgage to Cook.

But the story gets stranger. The next year, when Williams's payment was due, he stalled. Instead of simply saying that he couldn't pay, he concocted an elaborate story that he was owned a large sum of money from a very prominent "plantation owner" who lived in the South. He even produced a letter to verify his claim. Williams took his farce a bit farther and convinced the frail Alonzo Cook to travel from Ancram to Arkansas to pick up the money for him.

Sadly, Alonzo Cook received a severe blow to the head by trusting the wrong man. In the early morning hours of June 17, Cook died from a single blow to the head produced by a heavy object. Whatever the instrument was, it did the job and split Cook's skull clean open. The investigator, Dr. Robert Bowerhan of Copake, pronounced him dead. Coroner Dewey Lawrence of Hudson was the official who made the preliminary determination with the state police, and Columbia County sheriff Milton was certain that although Cook's charred body was pulled out of his burning apartment by the Ancram Fire Department, he had not died from smoke inhalation. Arson was confirmed by the strong odor of kerosene in Alonzo's bedroom. Even the telephone lines were cut to prevent the housekeeper from calling for help.

No one doubted that poor Alonzo Cook had been murdered. When the sheriff arrived on the scene, he immediately questioned Mr. and Mrs. Oakley, yet they hadn't seen a thing. When she discovered the smoke, however, she immediately went to the phone to call the fire department, only to find the phone was dead. When they turned to Captain Williams for answers, he, too, said he saw nothing.

When word spread about Alonzo's tragic death, a net was cast around the area in search of suspicious persons or newly paroled criminals. By chance, the stylish, fifty-eight-year-old sea captain Williams was investigated on the night of the murder on the slight chance that he'd forgotten a small detail or uncovered a relevant fact. Within hours, the captain shocked everyone by admitting to smashing Alonzo in the head with a Billy club, soaking him in kerosene, lighting his body on fire and cutting the telephone lines. To distract from the body, Williams set fires in other parts of the farm to draw attention away from his atrocious act. He confessed to authorities that he killed poor Alonzo Cook because they argued about what was owed on the $27,000 mortgage on the farm. The murder weapon was later discovered on the attic stairs, smeared with blood.

The papers called it the "hammer slaying." What was revealed after Williams was arraigned in front of Judge William E.J. Connor for first-degree murder was perhaps even more shocking. Williams had never been a graduate of Annapolis. In fact, he had only briefly served in the navy; he was court-martialed for impersonating an officer. In 1927, he did time in Arkansas—twenty-five years for grand larceny, robbery, arson and committing a bank heist. While on parole in 1934, Williams was arrested again on a similar charge of larceny. This time it wasn't a bank holdup, but rather the pilfering of two mules. Back in jail to serve his twenty-five years, Williams was miraculously discharged in 1942. Apparently, Steven Williams wasn't a guy who learned his lesson. Soon after the discharge, he joined the U.S. Maritime Service and rose to the rank of chief engineer, but he was again discharged for poor performance. Never returning his uniform, Williams, the imposter, continued to dress as a four-stripe officer and tell false tales of bravery.

On November 29, Steven Williams pleaded guilty to second-degree murder. He was sentenced to twenty-five years to life at Clinton Prison in Dannemora, New York. Although he appealed his conviction seven years later, it was denied. Williams never made it out of prison.

BIBLIOGRAPHY

Books

Bernstein, Nina. *The Lost Children of Wilder: The Epic Struggle to Change Foster Care*. Reprint. New York: Vintage Books, 2002.

Callan, Albert. *The Man in the Black Hat: Collected Columns from the* Chatham Courier. Chatham, NY: Hollis Publishing Company, 2003.

Child, Hamilton. *Gazetteer and Business Directory of Columbia County, N.Y. for 1871–2*. Hudson, NY: self-published, 1871.

Crockett, David. *The Life of Martin Van Buren*. New York: Nafis and Cornish, 1845.

Ellis, Captain Franklin. *The History of Columbia County, New York*. Philadelphia, PA: Everts L&L Ensign, 1878.

Hannaford, Phoebe Ann. *Daughters of America: Women of the Century*. Augusta, ME: True and Company, 1883.

Lankevich, George J. *River of Dreams: The Hudson Valley in Historic Postcards*. New York: Fordham University Press.

Leath, James Edward, and the Columbia County Historical Society. *Old House Speaks*. New York: Columbia County Historical Society, 1947.

Lossing, Benson J. *The Hudson: From the Wilderness to the Sea*. New York: Virtue and Yorston, 1866.

Mancall, Peter C. *Fatal Journey: The Final Expedition of Henry Hudson*. New York: Basic Books, 2010.

Marine Research Society Salem Massachusetts. *The Pirates Own Book, or Authentic Narratives of the Lives, Exploits, and Executions of the Most Celebrated Sea Robbers*. Salem, MA: self-published, 1924.

Mathews, C.S. *Mysterious Beauty: Living with the Paranormal in the Hudson Valley*. N.p.: Gatekeeper Press, 2019.

McNamee, Daniel Vincent. *Columbia County in the World War*. Albany, NY: J.B. Lyon Company Printers, 1924.

Munsell, Frank, and Patrick Thomas Hughes. *American Ancestry: Giving the Name and Descent in the Mail Line of Americans Whose Ancestors Settled in the United States Previous to the Declaration of Independence. A.D. 1776*. Albany, NY: J. Munsell's Sons, Publisher, 1887.

Raymond, William. *Biographical Sketches of the Distinguished Men of Columbia County, NY, Including an Account of the Most Important Offices They Have Filled in the State and General Governments, and in the Army and Navy*. Albany, NY: Weed, Parsons and Company, 1851.

Selzer, Adam. *Ghosts of Lincoln: Discovering His Paranormal Legacy*. Woodbury, MN: Llewellyn Publications, 2015.

Smith, H.P. *Columbia County at the End of the Century: A Historical Record of Its Formation and Settlements, Its Resources, Its Institutions, Its Industries and Its people*. Hudson, NY: Record Printing and Publishing Company, 1900.

Smith, J.E.A. *Taghconic: The Romance and Beauty of the Hills*. Boston: Lee and Shepard. 1879.

Spencer, Alfred. *Roster of Native Sons (and Daughters)*. N.p.: Courier Press, 1941.

Stanton, Henry. *Random Recollections*. New York, 1886.

Streisand, Barbra. *My Name Is Barbra*. New York: Viking, 2023.

Swanson, James L. *Bloody Crimes*. New York: William Morrow, 2010.

Von Behr, H.A. *Ghosts in Residence*. Utica, NY: North Country Books, 1993.

Articles

Albany Daily Evening Times. "Waiting for the Train." March 23, 1872.

Albany Times Union. Saturday, July 3, 1920.

The Argus. September 8, 1912.

Brooklyn Daily Eagle. January 10, 1910.

Campbell, Bill. "Cords and Discords." *Albany Times-Union*, December 25, 1944.

Chatham Courier. "Columbia County in 1800." September 20, 1979.

———. "A Dinosaur Grows in Churchtown." August 16, 1962.

———. "Elephant Farm Sold at Ghent." June 2, 1960.

———. February 6, 1947.

———. "The Hero of Cedar Creek." May 24, 1964.

———. July 9, 1959.

———. June 29, 1933.

———. "Lost Hunter Says Black Panther Trailed him in Austerlitz Woods." November 4, 1955.

———. May 1, 1947.

———. 1933.

———. "Ninety Years Ago, Abe Lincoln Passed Through Chatham on His Way to Albany." February 20, 1947.

———. "The Old Black Hat: When Old Chatham Was Young." September 22, 2005.

———. "Poems of Mary Chase Are Voice of Nature's Beauty." August 30, 1934.

———. "Riders Will Go Forth in Search of Thieves. 148th Meeting of Society for the Detection of Thieves, Will See 'Riders' Mounted as a Test of Their Equestrian Abilities." January 23, 1947.

———. "Tales of Old Columbia County: Federal Stores Once Prospered in Old Chatham." June 10, 1968.

Columbia Republican (Hudson, NY). July 17, 1902.

———. "Was an Example to All Slackers." July 10, 1917.

Daily Sentinel (Rome, NY). "Jonas Builds Dinosaurs for '64 Fair." August 26, 1963.

Davis, Christopher West. "An Island of American History." *New York Times*, July 21, 2002.

Gazette Courier (Greenfield, MA). "From Ward H. Lamon's Biography, Abraham Lincoln, His Personal Appearance." July 22, 1872.

Grimsley, Will. "30 Years Ago Saranzen Fired 'Miracle Shot.'" *Albany (NY) Knickerbocker News*, 1966.

Hudson (NY) Evening Register. "Famous Van Wormer Murder Trial Underway Here Forty Years Ago." April 3, 1942.

———. May 13, 1916.

Joray, Peter. "Poems of Mary Chase Are Voice of Nature's Beauty." *Chatham Courier*, August 30, 1934.

The Kinderhook (Sentinel, NY). 1842.

Lebanon Echo. August 4, 1942.

Mynter, Kenneth. "Their Land Gone, Less than 100 Indians Were in Columbia County." *Chatham Courier*, May 10, 1951.

New York Daily Tribune. "SUSAN WARNER. The Story of the Author of 'The Wide, Wide World.'" January 8, 1910.

New York Times. "Queechy House Is a Literary Shrine." July 21, 2002.

Post Standard (Syracuse, NY). April 18, 1902.

Schenectady Gazette. "Jonas' Wildlife Sculpture in Big Demand." October 3, 1983.

Shulman, Jim. "Baby Boomer Memories: Show Boat Was a Landlocked Landmark that Rocked." *Berkshire Eagle*, September 15, 2016.

Smith, D.S. Compton. "Captain Kidd." *Clinton Courier*, April 4, 1861,

Van Valkenburgh Williams, Katherine Fitch. *Chatham Courier*, November 1927.

Miscellaneous

Coggeshall, William Turner. "Lincoln Memorial: The Journeys of Abraham Lincoln from Springfield to Washington, 1861, as President Elect; and from Washington to Springfield, 1865, as President Martyred, 1824–1967." *Ohio State Journal*.

National Park Service. *Return to His Native Town: Martin Van Buren's Life at Lindenwald, 1839–1862.* History Program.

Paine, Laura. "Hands to Work, Hearts to God: The Story of the Shaker Seed Industry." PDF. HortTechnology, October–December 1993.

Websites

Allain, Shannon McCloskey. "The Summery Night Before the Frost." Open Letters Monthly. https://www.openlettersmonthlyarchive.com/olm/the-summery-night-before-the-frost.

Association for the Preservation of the Coelacanth. "Giant Dinosaurs Seen on Hudson, Headed for the City." https://gombessa.tripod.com/imagelib/sitebuilder/misc/show_image.html?linkedwidth=actual&linkpath=https://gombessa.tripod.com/sitebuildercontent/sitebuilderpictures/dinopress.jpg&target=tlx_new.

Columbia County Lutherans. "The Founding of the Congregation and Earliest Years to 1830." https://columbiacountylutherans.wordpress.com/st-thomas-churchtown-ny.

Country Dance & Song Society. "Supplication in a Nation's Calamity." YouTube videos available. https://cdss.org/publications/watch/songs-that-speak/supplication-in-a-nations-calamity.

Country School Association of America. "Little Red Schoolhouse." September 2006. https://csaa.typepad.com/country_school_associatio/2006/09/the_little_red_.html.

Dorman, Larry. "Gene Sarazen, 97, Golf Champion." *New York Times*, May 14, 1999. https://www.nytimes.com/1999/05/14/sports/gene-sarazen-97-golf-champion-dies.html.

Encyclopedia. "Sarazen, Gene." https://www.encyclopedia.com/humanities/encyclopedias-almanacs-transcripts-and-maps/sarazen-gene.

Evening World (New York). "Write Farewell Letters." September 30, 1903. Library of Congress. https://www.loc.gov/resource/sn83030193/1903-09-30/ed-1/?sp=1&q=kinderhook%2C+NY&r=-0.123,0.59,0.532,0.218,0.

Food52. "How the Sundae Got Its Name & the Origin of the Banana Split." Blog. https://food52.com/blog/16801-how-the-sundae-got-its-name-the-origin-of-the-banana-split.

Fowler, Henry, ed. *Mary M. Chase and Her Writings*. Boston: Ticknor and Fields, 1855. https://books.google.com.

Greener Pastures. "Chatham, New York, 1900." https://greenerpasture. com/Places/ShowNews/41639.

Hawthorne Valley Farmscape Ecology Program. "Columbia County/NYC Interactions: Flows of Nature, Agriculture, Ideas & People." https:// hvfarmscape.org/ecological-habitats-communities-columbia-county.

Historians of CC NY. "Town of Taghkanic." https://historian. columbiacountyny.com/municipal-historians/town-of-taghkanic.

Historical Sketches of Hudson. https://archive.org/details/ historicalsketch00mill/page/4/mode/2up?ref=ol&view=theater.

Koehl, Dan. "Adele Nelson Elephant Act." Elephant Encyclopedia, 2023. https://www.elephant.se/location2.php?location_id=721.

Library of Congress. "Bruce on the Stand: Murder of Hallenbeck Described by One Accused Man." https://www.loc.gov/ resource/sn83030214/1902-04-15/ed-1/?sp=9&q=valatie &r=-0.003,0.245,0.639,0.262,0.

Louis Paul Jonas. https://www.jonasstudios.com/studio_contents/ JonasBookProspectus.pdf.

Mallon, Thomas. "Hustler with a Lyric Voice: Edna St. Vincent Millay Combined a Modern Sensibility with Traditional Forms." *The Atlantic* (October 2001). https://www.theatlantic.com/magazine/ archive/2001/10/hustler-with-a-lyric-voice/302309.

Mercuri, Joanna. "Scholar Traces Evangelical Anti-Intellectualism to 19th-Century Reading Habits." Fordham Now, January 8, 2015. https:// news.fordham.edu/arts-and-culture/the-story-behind-it-all-scholar-traces-evangelical-anti-intellectualism-to-19th-century-reading-habits.

Mulvey, Susan J., trans. Miscellaneous Newspaper Articles, Columbia County, New York. US Gennet. http://www.usgennet.org/usa/ny/ county/columbia/newspapers/misc_articles.htm.

New York State Parks. "Park History Excelsior Conservation Corps: A Modern Vision of an Old Idea." January 12, 2016. https://nystateparks. blog/tag/great-depression.

New York Supreme Court, Appellate Division. https://www.google.com/ books/edition/Public_Papers/OIc-AAAAYAAJ?hl=en&gbpv=1&dq=n ew+york+appellate+court+division+van+wormer+trial+hallenbeck&p g=PA143&printsec=frontcover.

New York World's Fair, 1964/1965. "The Dinosaurs Come to the Fair." http://www.nywf64.com/sinclair08.html.

Pratt, Sam. "Cigar Stumps, Careless Tongues, Secret Ceremonies, Slave Labor and the South Bay." January 5, 2012. https://www.sampratt.com/sam/2012/01/prison.html.

Research Guides at Southern Adventist University. "Angelica Van Buren, First Lady for a Widower." First Ladies of the United States. libguides.com.

Teenage Film. "The New York State Training School for Girls, 1904–1975." October 17, 2013. https://www.teenagefilm.com/archives/archive-fever/the-new-york-state-training-school-for-girls-1904-1975/%20.

Wheeler, Peter. *Chains and Freedom: or The Life and Adventures of Peter Wheeler, A Colored Man Yet Living. A Slave in Chains, A Sailor on the Deep, And a Sinner at the Cross. Three Volumes in One by the Author of The Mountain Wild Flower.* Transcribed by Charles Edwards Lester, 1815–90. Documenting the American South. https://docsouth.unc.edu/neh/lester/lester.html.

Wikimedia Commons. https://commons.wikimedia.org.

William G. Pomeroy Foundation. "Peter Wheeler Historical Marker." https://www.wgpfoundation.org/historic-markers/peter-wheeler.

Zeigler, Lisa. "Naming Names: The Punishment of Girlhood." *Book and Room*. http://www.bookandroom.com/blog/2019/3/9/testament-of-youth-the-punishment-of-girlhood.

ABOUT THE AUTHOR

Allison is a graduate of Fordham University in New York City with a degree in communications and creative writing. She spent much of her professional career in public relations in New York and has traveled throughout the world promoting health and fitness resorts. In her work as a writer, Allison has written plays and movie reviews, as well as short fiction, articles and essays on local people, places and history in her adopted home of Columbia County, New York. Allison is the author of *Hidden History of Columbia County, New York* (The History Press, 2014) and *Hudson Valley Curiosities* (The History Press, 2017). Inspired by her deep research into the history of Columbia County, Allison now creates folk art paintings on reclaimed antique barn board reflecting the area's rural landscapes, weathered barns and historic sites.

Visit us at
www.historypress.com